ORY

# The Dutch Revolt
## 1559–1648

### Peter Limm

**LONGMAN**
London and New York

Addison Wesley Longman Limited
*Edinburgh Gate, Harlow,*
*Essex CM20 2JE, England*
*and Associated Companies throughout the world.*

Published in the United States of America
by Addison Wesley Longman Inc., New York.

*First published in 1989*
*Fifth impression 1997*

*Set in 10/11 point Baskerville (Linotron)*
*Produced through Longman Malaysia, GPS*

ISBN 0 582 35594 X

To Katie and Andrew

---

**British Library Cataloguing in Publication Data**
Limm, Peter
 The Dutch revolt 1559–1648. – (Seminar
 studies in history).
 1. Netherlands. War with Spain, 1568–1648
 I. Title  II. Series
 949.203

 ISBN 0-582-35594-X

**Library of Congress Cataloging-in-Publication Data**
Limm, Peter.
 The Dutch revolt, 1559–1648/Peter Limm.
  p.   cm. — (Seminar studies in history)
 Bibliography: p.
 Includes index.
 ISBN 0-582-35594-X
 1. Netherlands — History — Wars of Independence, 1556–1648.
I. Title.  II. Series.
DH186.L56  1989
949.2'02 — dc 19                                    88-38542
                                                         CIP

# Contents

*Contents*

# List of maps

# A note on currency

The Dutch coinage mentioned in the text has been converted to *florins* of 20 *pattards* (the principal money of account in the Netherlands). There were about 10 *florins* to the pound sterling in the later sixteenth century; 2 *florins* to the *ducat* and 2 *florins* to the *escudo*.

In Castile in the sixteenth century accounts were kept in *ducats*. One *ducat* was worth 375 *maravedis* (an older basic unit of account). In the seventeenth century 34 *maravedis* made up a *real* (standard silver coin of circulation). The *escudo* was another Spanish gold coin of circulation worth 10 *reales*.

# Acknowledgements

We are grateful to the following for permission to reproduce copyright material:
Maps redrawn from: *Europe and the Decline of Spain* by R. A. Stradling, published by George Allen & Unwin 1981 and *The Dutch Republic and the Hispanic World* by J. I. Israel, published by Oxford University Press 1982 © J. I. Israel 1982.

Cover: Statue of Alva in the citadel of Antwerp. He is trampling upon Dutch rebels. From Baudart: *Les Guerres de Nassau*, 1616.

# Seminar Studies in History

## Introduction

The Seminar Studies series was conceived by Patrick Richardson, whose experience of teaching history persuaded him of the need for something more substantial than a textbook chapter but less formidable than the specialised full-length academic work. He was also convinced that such studies, although limited in length, should provide an up-to-date authoritative introduction to the topic under discussion as well as a selection of relevant documents and a comprehensive bibliography.

Patrick Richardson died in 1979, but by that time the Seminar Studies series was firmly established, and it continues to fulfil the role he intended for it. This book, like others in the series, is therefore a living tribute to a gifted and original teacher.

*Note on the System of References*:
A bold number in round brackets (**5**) in the text refers the reader to the corresponding entry in the Bibliography section at the end of the book. A bold number in square brackets, preceded by 'doc.' [**doc. 6**] refers the reader to the corresponding item in the section of Documents, which follows the main text.

Words with an asterisk beside them are defined in the Glossary on page 135.

# Part One:   The Background

## 1   Historical Background

In 1627 the Spanish councillor of state Fernando Giron considered
the struggle between the Spanish crown and its rebels in the Low
Countries to be 'the biggest, bloodiest and most implacable of all
the wars which have been waged since the beginning of the world'
(**28**, p. 58). By that date the war had already lasted sixty years and
still had another twenty to run. There was continuous fighting
from April 1572 to April 1607 (apart from a cease-fire of six
months' duration in 1577) and from April 1621 to June 1647. Yet
as one historian has written recently: 'There can no longer be
any doubt that the Spanish crown had come to accept the prin-
ciple of Dutch political and religious independence by 1606, and
that there was never subsequently any Spanish ambition or
plan for reconquering the break-away northern Netherlands'
(**54**, p. xiv). Why, then, did the war continue for as long as it
did?

Jonathan Israel thinks the answer is that 'there were strong
contradictory pressures towards war and peace in both the
Republic and Spain and these contradictory tendencies derived
from political and economic circumstances intimately linked to the
major problems of the Republic and Spain' (**54**, p. xv). A modern
account of the Spanish-Dutch conflict thus has to identify the
major issues and problems facing Spain and the Netherlands in the
sixteenth and seventeenth centuries and then to set those issues
and problems in their proper context.

Many accounts of the revolt have adopted an unduly narrow
nationalistic or religious stance. Only recently has the revolt been
set more appropriately in an international context. Geoffrey Parker
has shown how the revolt became the focal point for other European struggles and developments, so that especially after 1572 the
conflict came to influence the policies of England, France, the
German princes and even the Ottoman Sultan. He has suggested
that after 1598 revolt developed further into a global conflict: 'The
Dutch Revolt, which began among a few thousand refugees in
north-western Europe ... spread until it affected the lives of

The Low Countries, 1566–1648

0    50    100    150 km

EAST
FRIESLAND
● Emden

GRONINGEN

Ems

FRIESLAND
TERRITORY
OF DRENTE

● Lingen

IJssel

OVERIJSSEL

● Oldenzaal

● Enkhuizen
● Hoorn

HOLLAND

● Haarlem    ● Amsterdam

● Deventer

UTRECHT    GELDERLAND

● Leiden

● Grol

The Hague ●    ● Delft    ● Utrecht

Rhine

● Arnhem

Schenkenschans

Rotterdam ●

Waal    ● Nijmegen    ● Cleves

● Rees

ZEALAND

● Dordrecht

● Wesel

's Hertogenbosch

Gennep ●

Rheinberg ●

● Middelburg

● Breda    ● Eindhoven

Geldern    ● Orsoy

Flushing ●

Bergen-op-Zoom

● Venlo

Zandvliet

● Brugge    Hulst

● Antwerp

Roermond ●    Düsseldorf ●

Ostend ●

Sas van Gent

BRABANT    ● Maastricht

● Dunkirk

Ghent ●

● Mechelen

LIÈGE

● Julich

FLANDERS

Lys    Scheldt

● Leuven

LIMBURG

WALLOON
FLANDERS

TOURNAI    ● Brussels

● Lille

HAINAUT

NAMUR

● Liège

ARTOIS

CAMBRAI

● Arras

Sambre

LUXEMBOURG

Meuse

■ Spanish Netherlands

▨ Independent Bishopric of Liège

▤ Territories conquered or reconquered
  by the Dutch 1626–48

millions of people and . . . [became] . . . so to say, the First World War' (**81**, pp. 62–3).

Not surprisingly, such a war raises a number of questions for the student of early modern Europe. Why did the struggle take place? How and why did it develop? What were the calculations and objectives of the contestants and their neighbours? Finally, what were the economic, social, military and political consequences? This book will attempt to answer these questions.

## The Habsburgs and the Burgundian inheritance

The heartland of the duchy of Burgundy lay in eastern France around Dijon. When the last of the Capetian dukes of the duchy died without heirs in 1361, it reverted to King John II of France. However, the circumstances of the Hundred Years' War (1338–1453) between England and France resulted in John's imprisonment in England: he assigned Burgundy as an apanage to his fourth son, Philip the Bold. There were dangers for John in this situation, and although Philip regarded himself as loyal to France he nevertheless pursued a policy of territorial expansion. Through marriage, family alliances and war Philip managed to acquire Flanders, Artois and also Franche Comté (known as the Free County of Burgundy, which adjoined his duchy). After Philip's death in 1404 his successors continued to expand Burgundian authority by further matchmaking, diplomacy, and war, so that by 1467, following the acquisition of Holland, Zealand Hainaut, Mechelen (or Malines), Limburg and Luxembourg, the centre of gravity of the duchy moved towards the north-west. Brussels became the new ducal capital.

Nevertheless, the dukes ruled over not so much a state but a miscellaneous collection of counties, duchies, city-states and prince-bishoprics which individually owed them allegiance. What was needed was an administrative framework to centralise ducal authority and to create a sense of unity. Charles the Rash (1467–77) planned to remedy this situation by taking control of the various territories which separated Franche-Comté and the Netherlands and turning the enlarged Burgundy into an independent kingdom. Unity and the achievement of royal status were his aims.

However, the duke's enemies joined forces to defeat and kill him at the battle of Nancy (1477). The original duchy of Burgundy reverted by feudal law to Louis XI, leaving the provinces of the

3

Netherlands and Franche-Comté to Charles's widow, Margaret. Louis XI had plans for controlling the entire inheritance and invaded Franche-Comté, Artois, Boulogne and Flanders. This forced Margaret, with the approval of the Netherlands States-General, to declare war and to seek outside help by marrying her daughter, Mary, to the Austrian archduke (and future emperor), Maximilian of Habsburg. Both Margaret and Mary had to promise the cities and provinces of the Netherlands (by way of a 'Grand Privilege'), that their 'liberties', separate customs and laws would be guaranteed. In this way the northern areas of the old duchy of Burgundy were saved from absorption by France. However, the marriage and the 'Grand Privilege' weakened ducal control.

By marrying Maximilian, Mary linked the fortunes of Burgundy with those of the house of Habsburg and although this alliance proved sufficient to force Louis XI to renounce his claims to the Netherlands provinces of Burgundy, it did not prevent him retaining control of the old duchy lands around Dijon. Furthermore, although the 'Habsburg Netherlands' was officially recognised by France in 1482, Maximilian soon realised that Mary's 'Grand Privilege' and other charters had undermined her father's attempts to centralise ducal authority and to create effective institutions of government. The traditionally narrow and highly conservative particularism of the states of the Netherlands had been given a boost. This was significant since Habsburg rule was eventually to founder on the rock of local particularism which expressed itself in the cry of 'defence of liberties'.

'Defence of liberties' became a demand for the preservation of traditional ways of doing things which served the interests of the wealthier sections of society: it was also a demand by traditional rulers for a share in government. When the Habsburgs challenged these 'liberties' they aroused great resentment among the richer subjects, a resentment bordering on rebellion. When such resistance was fused with a struggle for religious toleration and a greater degree of freedom by those lower down the social pyramid, the Habsburgs faced an acute crisis of government in the Netherlands which eventually led the seven most northern provinces (the 'United Provinces') to renounce Spanish sovereignty altogether and to create the Dutch Republic. How did this crisis come about?

# The extension of Habsburg power

Mary died in 1482 but not before giving birth to two children, one of whom, Philip (b. 1478), was recognised by Louis as ruler of the Netherlands in the treaty of Arras (also 1482). However, Philip was only a baby, and Maximilian claimed the right to act as regent. Many of the towns resisted this move because they feared Maximilian would erode their 'liberties'. After a protracted civil war in which he had to use imperial troops against Brugge (Bruges), Maximilian regained popular support and control of Franche Comte and Artois. Yet in 1493 Maximilian left the Netherlands to become Emperor, leaving the fifteen-year-old Duke Philip in control.

Philip maintained Habsburg rule in the Netherlands (1493–1506) by reviving the process of centralising administration and by keeping on terms with the States-General. In 1496 he married Juana of Castile, a Spanish princess. Juana gave birth to a son, Charles of Ghent, but when he inherited the Burgundian inheritance on the death of his father in 1506 he was only six years old. The real ruler was Margaret, widow of the Duke of Savoy (regent 1507–15).

However, when Charles came of age in 1515 and took over the reins of government, there was little opposition. Having spent all his life in the Netherlands he was a popular figure, especially as he followed the advice of the lord of Chièvres and avoided antagonising the regents of the towns. However, in 1516, on the death of his grandfather, Ferdinand, he became King Charles I of Spain and, three years later, was elected Charles V, Holy Roman Emperor. Suddenly his Burgundian interests were relegated in his list of priorities and after 1517, when he left for Spain, Margaret governed the Netherlands for him as regent once again (1518–30), to be followed by his own sister, Mary (regent 1531–55).

Charles had planned to regain control of the old duchy of Burgundy from France (**92**) and as a first step towards this end he acquired Tournai in 1521 and Cambrai in 1543, and forced the French to renounce their claims to Flanders. Although Charles ultimately failed to achieve his ambition, he nevertheless revived the expansionist policies of earlier dukes and the process of developing central institutions to unify his government and administration. He extended his authority over the lands of the north-east Netherlands: Friesland was annexed in 1523–4; Utrecht and Overijssel in 1528; Groningen, the Ommelanden and Drenthe in

1536; and Gelderland and Zutphen in 1543. Thus by 1548 Charles controlled seventeen provinces in the Netherlands: Holland, Zealand, Brabant, Flanders, Walloon Flanders, Artois, Luxembourg, Hainaut, Mechelen, Namur, Groningen and Ommelanden (combined), Friesland, Gelderland, Limburg, Tournai, Utrecht, Overijssel and Drenthe (combined). Cambrai remained part of the Holy Roman Empire until 1678 (see map, p. 2).

On 26 June 1548 Charles persuaded the Diet of the Holy Roman Empire (in the 'Augsburg Transaction') to allow him to make all his Netherlands territories which formed part of the Empire into a separate administrative unit. Thus provinces ruled by Charles V in the Netherlands became virtually independent of the Empire. In order to guarantee Habsburg control over these territories, Charles persuaded the States of each province to accept a 'Pragmatic Sanction' (November 1549), which ensured that following the Emperor's death, all seventeen provinces would accept the same central institutions and, more importantly, the same ruler: Charles's son, Philip. There were only a few exceptions. Along with Cambrai, the provinces of Liege and Ravenstein and parts of Gelderland remained entirely free of Habsburg control (**19**). In Brabant the duke of Aerschot, head of the house of Croy, retained his right to do fealty only to the duke of Brabant. However, while the Pragmatic Sanction provided Charles with the opportunity to consolidate his Netherlands territories and to institutionalise his authority, it did not guarantee unity or unquestioning obedience.

## The structure of government

By the mid-sixteenth century, all seventeen provinces of the Netherlands obeyed the orders of the Brussels government and recognised the same ruler. When Charles was absent from the country the provinces recognised his representative as regent. This government consisted of a Council of State for high policy, a Council of Finance for fiscal affairs and a Privy Council for justice. There were law courts (or 'councils') in each province and a supreme court, or 'great council', at Mechelen. In every province there was a Stadholder appointed by the ruler to ensure that his orders were put into effect (**80**).

However, the ruler of the Netherlands did not have a single title such as 'Grand Duke' or 'King'. Charles was called 'Duke of Brabant, Limbourg, Luxembourg and Gelderland, Count of Flanders, Artois, Hainaut, Holland, Zealand and Namur, Lord of Friesland and Mechelen'. This emphasised the fact that the Netherlands was a loose confederation of parts. Every province and most of the smaller areas had a representative assembly – the 'States' (*staten* or local parliaments). These usually included delegates from the nobility, the clergy, and the leading towns, though they were not democratically chosen and sometimes one of the three orders might not be represented at all. Yet the States were powerful. They could raise troops and levy and collect taxes and they kept a watching brief on the constitution. They were the main defence of local liberties.

The local States sent delegates to attend the States-General (or general parliament) which negotiated directly with the ruler or regent. Each delegation had to refer back to the local States for advice on any measure and there had to be unanimous agreement before deputies could communicate their decision to the States-General. Furthermore, all the provinces had to approve a measure before it could be enacted. Hence decision-making was a slow process. It was not helped by the fact that the States-General only met every three years, and sometimes there had to be a number of meetings before the necessary unanimity was achieved. Until 1549 only the hereditary provinces of the house of Burgundy were allowed to attend, but after that date this right was extended to all those provinces who had assented to the Augsburg Transaction of 1548. Over some issues a certain amount of cooperation between representatives could be achieved, though it would be wrong to exaggerate this. Often, as we shall see, States used 'defence of liberties' to mask inter-province rivalry, even rivalry between cities within a province. Thus, although under Charles Netherlanders began to speak of their *patrie* or Fatherland, many states retained a selfishness which seriously undermined the development of corporate status (**95**).

The Habsburgs, and the Burgundians before them, had always seen the value of securing the loyalty of the high nobility and had granted a number of aristocratic families special privileges such as high-ranking positions in the church, local government and the army. The most eminent of them were elected to the prestigious Order of the Golden Fleece and were consulted on both domestic and foreign affairs in the Council of State. Under Mary, when the Council of State was rarely convoked, government was often conducted by way of a series of informal consultations with selected members. Charles V followed the advice of his secretary Nicholas

Perrenot, lord of Granvelle (father of the more famous cardinal), who stated in a memorandum to his master in 1531:

> 'It seems that it would be good that, of the great nobles whom it shall please the emperor to appoint to the said Council of State, two or three should always reside continuously near the ... queen to assist her. They should be persons most suitable for her service ... That when matters of importance arise, all the knights of the Order [of the Golden Fleece] should be summoned'.

However, Philip II's policies were to undermine the consultative role of the high nobility and reduce its share of government. As will be seen later, the nobles reacted strongly to this threat. Their rebellion served to encourage the centrifugal force of particularism and to act as a catalyst for a number of other divisive influences.

## Other divisive influences

The map of the Netherlands (p. 2) shows that Charles V's provinces covered a large area (34,000 square miles), but that there were many physical obstacles impeding communications between them. The provinces of Holland, Zealand, Utrecht and Friesland were practically surrounded by the sea and cut off from the 'heartland provinces' of Hainaut, Artois, Flanders and Brabant, by numerous rivers, dykes, and lakes. The eastern and north-eastern provinces of Limburg, Luxembourg, Gelderland, Overijssel, Drenthe and Groningen were cut off from the rest by dunes, bogs and heaths and by the independent principality of Liège. Owen Feltham, an English traveller in the Netherlands in 1652, described the area as being 'The great Bog of Europe ... it is the buttock of the World, full of veines and bloud, but no bones in't' [**doc. 1**].

This quagmire often made horse-and-cart transport impossible. The usual route from Friesland to the south was by boat, but this form of transport was not very quick. Only twenty-five miles separated Breda from 's Hertogenbosch but it still took about eight hours to go from one to the other. In the south communications were better, and letters from Antwerp could reach Ghent or Brussels in a day. In terms of time-distance, as Parker has pointed out, 'Brussels and Antwerp were ... closer to Paris and Cologne than they were to Amsterdam and Groningen' (**80**, p. 22). More significantly for later events, the postal courier took between two and three weeks to reach Spain. Small wonder, then, that there were strong local institutions and traditions in the Netherlands and little sense of unity between the provinces.

There were different legal and fiscal systems and different linguistic areas. There were about 700 different legal codes in the Netherlands, and it was quite possible to avoid punishment by crossing into a different province. Even within a province codes could vary from town to town (the province of Artois had 248 separate legal codes). Yet Netherlanders were prepared to live with the illogicality of this system because they valued the existence of guaranteed privileges above administrative convenience. When governments threatened local liberties revolts could occur. Brussels and 's Hertogenbosch both defied the government in 1523–5; Ghent rebelled in 1539–40 (though it lost its privileges as a result); there was rioting in Antwerp in 1554; and many of the newly-conquered north-eastern provinces (especially Gelderland), were never happy under Habsburg control (**19**).

Charles V was a warrior king (as much by necessity as by design) and as a result he incurred a mounting debt. The Netherlands had to pay dearly for his imperial commitments, but especially for the war which broke out against France in 1551. Many of the states were alarmed to see how the financial deficit in the Netherlands had risen inexorably from 415,878 Flemish pounds in 1531 to nearly 7,000,000 Flemish pounds in 1555 (**80**). One method Charles used to try and cut the deficit was to borrow on the Antwerp money market. Interest on loans was as high as 30 per cent and Charles often had to use his demesne lands as security. He also sought to increase taxation and this provoked considerable resentment.

However, it was Philip II who experienced the worst of the backlash to Charles V's fiscal policies in the Netherlands. At a meeting of the States-General in 1556, the deputies from Brussels opposed Philip's call for a new tax to continue the war. After an undignified quarrel, the States agreed to allow new taxes, but only on condition that they would supervise the collection and distribution of all money raised. Philip realised that the power to withhold money until grievances were redressed was a serious check to his authority, but in the circumstances there was no alternative. When peace was signed at Câteau-Cambresis in 1559 the Netherlanders were delighted because they expected a reduction in taxes. Philip II, however, was more concerned to re-establish Spanish authority in the Netherlands.

Another obstacle to unity in the Netherlands was linguistic individuality. Dutch was the predominant language, especially in the northern and central areas. It had two main forms, West Dutch and Oosters, although in the north another variety, Fries, was spoken. In the south, however, many people spoke a form of French called Walloon, although Picard and Flemish were other variants. In the east Low German was written and spoken. Although the eventual split between north and south did not follow linguistic boundaries these linguistic divisions helped to bolster political disunity and to encourage the negative aspects of particularism.

There were also social and economic tensions in the Netherlands in the first half of the sixteenth century. There were about 4,000 nobles in the Netherlands by the 1560s, and although there was a great spread of wealth and power within this group, there was a sense of cohesion and unity, especially in opposition to the towns. Many of the aristocracy, or 'grandees', were large landholders, often with international connections. The Orange-Nassau family had German, Italian and French relations (the principality of Orange was situated in southern France), and the families of Hornes and Egmont were related to the Montmorencies in France. Nevertheless, in the north the lesser nobility dominated the countryside, and many of these were only clients of the grandees with lifestyles little different from the richer peasants. Some lived in the towns and attempted to earn a living through trade and industry.

The inflation of the sixteenth century created many difficulties for both the higher and lower nobility. Most grandees refused to alter their lifestyle and reduce expenditure in the face of rising living costs. Many preferred to borrow money rather than appear to lose status, though they incurred great debts in this way. The nobles often demanded to be exempted from taxation to ease their financial worries, and this increased the opposition of the towns and of the urban patricians in particular.

The patricians (or 'regents') were mostly successful financiers and merchants. They dominated municipal town councils and jealously guarded their political and economic predominance. Lower down the urban social pyramid were guildsmen and shopkeepers, many of whom wanted to acquire patrician status. However, guildsmen were often annoyed by the way the patricians prevented all but the most successful and wealthy from joining their ranks, and in times of hardship some guildsmen joined with those lower down the social scale (labourers and casual workers) in uprisings against the patricians. The patricians, therefore, had a vested interest in organising and deploying the local forces of law and order to put down such protests, often in a brutal manner. Thus there were tensions between nobles and towns, and in the towns between patricians and other social groups. However, as well as tensions *within* towns, there was much rivalry *between* them.

By 1549 most of the three million inhabitants of the Netherlands lived in the western provinces of Holland, Zealand, Hainaut, Flanders and Brabant. In this area the Netherlands had the highest population density in Europe and most people lived in towns. In all there were 200 towns in the Netherlands, but those in the coastal provinces were the largest and wealthiest. This was because trade was of vital importance for the Netherlands and proximity to the sea was a great advantage.

Initially, Antwerp, the largest town with 80,000 inhabitants, was the main trading centre. Situated on the river Scheldt it handled 75 per cent of the total trade of the Netherlands, exporting local textiles and importing spices, salt and wool from Portugal and Spain, as well as English cloth, German metals and Italian luxury goods. This activity attracted other commercial and financial interests, so that Antwerp became northern Europe's main centre for currency-dealing and financial negotiations. The famous *Beurs* or Exchange was built in 1531 to house Antwerp's financial activities, and bankers from all over Europe used it to arrange loans or to speculate.

However, during the first half of the sixteenth century, Antwerp's position as the major trading centre of the Netherlands was threatened. Its trade with Portugal, Germany and England declined, and the towns of Holland, especially Amsterdam, Rotterdam and Haarlem, began to exploit their more favourable geographical position to trade with ports along the Baltic shore. Increasingly these seaboard towns provided the bulk of Dutch requirements for basic foodstuffs and cereals, wine, textiles, salt, metals and especially fish. Amsterdam, though much smaller than Antwerp, came to be very prosperous by the middle of the century and there was much rivalry between the two cities. Yet the commercial rise of Holland was in contrast to the experience of towns in the south (Ghent for example) and in the east. This generated both envy and jealousy of Holland's good fortune, a fact which was to have a bearing on later events (**111**).

Another serious challenge to unity in the Netherlands was provided by religious persecution. Charles V was a staunch Catholic, and early in his reign he determined that heresy should not be allowed to take root in the Netherlands. Many educated Netherlanders had accepted criticisms of the Catholic Church made by individuals like Desiderius Erasmus (1469–1536) or movements like the Brethren of the Common Life* and the *Devotio Moderna**. However, the Netherlands proved a fertile area for a confusing number of reformers and religious groups (**57**).

Religious ideas followed the merchants and traders from Germany and Switzerland, and Lutheranism soon reached the Netherlands, finding support both among the nobility and the townsfolk. Anabaptists* and their leader Menno Simmons gained support in Holland, Flanders, and Friesland. Followers of Martin Bucer in Strasburg and Heinrich Bullinger in Zurich developed their ideas in the Netherlands, and there were a host of other less well-known figures, such as David Joris, who claimed to be a new Messiah, and Hendrik Niclaes who founded a spiritualist community – the 'Family of Love'. There was little unity amongst these religious groups beyond a common rejection of the Catholic Mass, and of the role of the priest, and an insistence that the form of church organisation should have a Biblical foundation. A number of local authorities agreed with some of these ideas and were most reluctant to condemn these groups for holding heretical beliefs.

However, Charles V identified Lutheranism as a serious threat and he condemned it in the Netherlands (October 1520) before he did so in the rest of the Empire (Worms, 1521). He revived the local inquisition in 1522 and in July 1523 the first Protestant martyr was burned in Brussels. This was followed by further edicts in 1529 and 1531 proclaiming death for Lutherans. From 1550 the death sentence was mandatory for those who possessed a Protestant book or translation of the Bible, let alone for those who attended Protestant services. As Charles informed Mary, his regent, 'What is tolerated in Germany must never be suffered in the Netherlands'. At least 2,000 Protestant heretics were executed for their beliefs in the Netherlands during his reign, although almost two-thirds of them were Anabaptists*.

Nevertheless, this harsh treatment of Protestants kept heresy at bay. Protestantism could not develop a solid core of popular support or secure much protection from the nobility. Apart from in the larger towns, such as Antwerp, and in remote rural areas, Charles V succeeded in preserving the predominance of the Catholic Church. Yet there was a price to be paid for this success. The heresy laws undermined many established local rights and authorities. The inquisition claimed the right to arrest and try Protestants in all parts of the Netherlands, irrespective of the views of local magistrates. Despite the constant stream of accusations and condemnations, many magistrates often refused to prosecute offenders as a way of circumventing the powers of the 'foreign' inquisitors. Charles regularly threatened law officers in the provinces with a number of punishments if they obstructed the full application of the heresy laws, but often to no avail (**92, 93**).

The persecutions tended to drive the really committed into more radical groups. In the 1540s and 1550s the Mennonites (Anabaptist\* followers of Menno Simmons), gained many followers. They were considered to be a real threat to society even though they, like the Lutherans, stressed individual protest rather than organised resistance. Hence they were hounded down more assiduously than other groups. However, from the 1550s supporters of John Calvin (1509–64), the Genevan reformer, began to develop Calvinist communities in the Netherlands and attracted a number of those who refused to surrender to persecution. Calvinism introduced a pattern of church organisation and a number of ideas which could more readily be adapted for group resistance to lay authority. Even though Calvinism developed very slowly and never became the religion of the majority in the Netherlands, it was to play an important part in the revolt against Philip II (**7, 21**).

## A new ruler: continuity and change

From the beginning of the 1550s it was clear to his close advisers that Charles was unwell. Gout and insomnia often reduced him to tears and forced him to abdicate his Netherlands territories to Philip on 25 October 1555. Three months later, in January 1556, Charles abdicated all his Spanish dominions and in March 1556 Philip was proclaimed king of Spain. In May 1558, the year of his death, Charles formally abdicated the Empire and his brother, Ferdinand I, was elected his successor. Although Charles's vast Empire had been divided between the Spanish and Austrian branches of the Habsburg family, Philip II's control over Spain and the Netherlands ensured the continued influence of Spain in vital strategic areas of western Europe (**64, 97**).

There was also a basic continuity of political policy from Charles through Philip. In 1543 Charles had instructed Philip on his priorities as a regent: to serve God, uphold the inquisition, suppress heresy, dispense justice and hold the balance between advisers.

Charles also advised his son to pay particular attention to finance and to maintain his inheritance intact. Philip, like his father, regarded the Netherlands as his patrimony, an integral part of his inheritance which could never be given up. However, while Philip attempted to follow his father's advice, he could not react in exactly the same way as Charles to specific problems.

Philip continued his father's policy of persecuting heresy, and many Calvinists fled abroad to England, France or Germany. In his approach to government, however, Philip was less inclined than his father to compromise with traditional ruling groups in the Netherlands. He never made any attempt to speak Dutch or French, and he maintained a Spanish haughtiness which offended the grandees. They were particularly annoyed by the way he did not involve them in the business of government but instead relied on a small corps of trusted Spanish officials. He also tried to dominate the States-General without paying much heed to the privileges and interests of the deputies. It was as if Philip wanted to Hispanicise the Netherlands.

It is certainly true that Philip, like his father, believed that Spain, and especially Castile, was the centre of the Habsburg monarchy. It was of critical importance to him to keep Castile law-abiding and peaceful, for it was his chief source of men and money. In 1558 leading Spanish nobles, already exempt from taxation, precipitated a crisis of authority as they tried to wrest further privileges from their absentee king. There was a revolt in Aragon and indications that heresy might be developing in some cities. Even more important than these domestic issues was the problem of defence against the Ottoman Turks in the Mediterranean, and news that a Spanish army had been badly defeated near Oran was enough to persuade Philip that he had to return to Spain. As soon as peace was signed with France, Philip made plans to sail home. He left Brussels on 5 July 1559, never to return.

# Part Two: Descriptive Analysis

## 2 Prelude to Revolt, 1559–1566

Before leaving the Netherlands in 1559, Philip appointed his half-sister, Margaret of Parma, regent and governess-general. However, Philip wanted to retain all executive power in his own hands, so despite the fact that he arranged for Margaret to be advised by the Councils of State and Finance and the Privy Council, he still felt it necessary to appoint a small group of trustworthy Spanish 'advisers' to relay information to and from the Netherlands. Philip also ensured that Margaret's personal officials had close links with officials in Madrid (for example, her confidential secretary, Tomás de Armenteros, was the cousin of Philip's own secretary of state in Spain, Gonzalo Pérez).

The foremost minister and adviser was Antoine Perrenot, bishop of Arras and later Cardinal Granvelle. His father had been Charles V's leading councillor and Antoine had grown up at court. He gained the emperor's favour at a very young age, and this preferment annoyed many courtiers and grandees. They particularly resented Perrenot's domineering manner and the way he used government patronage to advance the interests of his family and friends. Although not a Spaniard by birth, the grandees soon came to consider Perrenot to be the eyes and ears of the king of Spain at Margaret's court. Many of the grandees had assumed that once Philip returned to Spain, they would act as the main source of advice for Margaret. When it became clear that this was not to happen, a number of them began to attack the Council of State and Granvelle in particular.

The most eminent of the noblemen who began to show disaffection with Philip's government in the Netherlands was William of Orange-Nassau. Born in 1533, William of Nassau was heir to the small German county of Nassau, but in 1544 he unexpectedly inherited the lands of the house of Orange in Brabant, Holland, Luxembourg, and Burgundy as well as the small principality of Orange in south-eastern France. As one of the greatest landowners in the Netherlands, William secured a place at Charles V's court while still a young man. When he was just twenty-three, Orange was appointed a Councillor of State by Philip II and at the same time he became a member of the exclusive Order of the Golden Fleece. During Philip II's period of residence in the Netherlands Orange was on good terms with Perrenot and accepted a number of favours from him. However, in August 1561 William married the daughter of Maurice of Saxony, an implacable enemy of the Habsburgs and the most powerful prince in Germany. Personal ambition was certainly an important motive for this political match. Orange's father had left the family fortunes in dire straits and the Saxon marriage brought William a handsome dowry and made him 'a person of international standing at a stroke' (**102**). Granvelle did all he could to sabotage Orange's plans, knowing that Philip II was against the marriage, and this made William an enemy of the Cardinal. When Orange persevered against Philip's express wishes he ruined his standing at court (**62**, Ch. 5).

Of the other leading nobles who showed unease about the new order in the Netherlands, Lamoral, count of Egmont, and Philippe de Montmorency, count Hornes, stand out. Egmont was ten years older than Orange and possessed extensive resources of patronage as governor of the provinces of Flanders, Walloon Flanders and Artois. Count Hornes, related to the powerful Montmorency family in France, had until 1561 been 'superintendent of Netherlands affairs' at Philip's court in Madrid, having travelled to Spain in 1559 as the king's personal bodyguard. However, Hornes disliked the way important decisions were taken without his advice and he returned to the Netherlands determined to undermine Granvelle's authority (**44**).

## Growing opposition: garrisons, Spanish councillors and bishoprics

Earlier, in 1560, the States of the southern provinces had successfully resisted one of Philip's plans for the Netherlands. The Spanish king had intended to garrison 3,000 Spanish troops in strategic towns along the southern frontier of the Netherlands. Philip claimed that the troops were needed to defend the Low Countries from French attack. The municipal authorities concerned claimed that the king was merely using the Netherlands as a useful colony to maintain Spanish influence in Lombardy, Sicily and Naples. In retaliation the local States refused to release funds to pay the soldiers. Soon the unpaid troops became restless and mutinous. Philip could ill-afford trouble in the Netherlands at this time, and he reluctantly instructed his troops to embark for Spain.

Orange and Egmont were critical of another of Philip's plans: his intention to appoint extra Spanish noblemen as Councillors of State. The two nobles had joined with the local States of the southern Netherlands in opposing the garrisoning of troops there, and when Philip abandoned his plans on that issue he also reluctantly agreed not to appoint more Spaniards as Councillors. To appease the nobility Philip appointed some of them to the important position of Stadholder. William of Orange, for instance, was made Stadholder of Holland, Zealand and Utrecht and in 1562 was made Stadholder of Franche-Comté. However, Perrenot was under no illusion that these victories for the nobles and States would terminate their campaign against the government and he was not surprised when they began to attack again in 1561, this time against Philip's new bishopric scheme.

Charles V had made a number of proposals to reform the ecclesiastical organisation of the Netherlands, but it was only in May 1559 that Philip and the Pope agreed on a scheme. This was to create fourteen new bishoprics to displace the foreign sees under whose jurisdiction the previous organisation had been placed. All the Netherlands was to be controlled by a primate of the Low Countries, the new archbishop of Mechelen. Significantly, the archibishopric of Mechelen was to be incorporated with the abbey of Afflighem in Brabant and the new appointment was to receive the abbot's revenues. A joint royal-papal committee decided that this method of financing was to be extended to the other new dioceses. Philip's scheme also stipulated that each new bishop had to be a doctor of theology and had to appoint two inquisitors to help monitor the ideas and behaviour of his flock.

When details of the scheme were finally made known in 1561, there was an instant reaction from influential groups in the Netherlands. The grandees were angry because Philip had kept the scheme secret from them for so long and they saw it as one more attempt to reduce their political influence at the regent's court. The existing abbots, and especially those in Brabant, were fearful that their influence in provincial assemblies would be undermined by the new abbot-bishops. They claimed that the scheme was an attempt to extend Spanish control of provincial parliaments and ecclesiastical affairs. The new recruits would, the abbots claimed, sit, act and vote as a Spanish pressure group.

This threat also united the nobility and the towns against the scheme. The nobles were alarmed that it might close down a profitable avenue of employment for their younger sons who had traditionally found careers for themselves in the church. The municipal authorities and the populace in general feared that the appointment of new inquisitors would herald a fresh round of religious persecution. The magistrates of Antwerp were particularly annoyed because a renewal of persecution threatened many profitable trading activities handled by heretics. Orange was especially angry when he learned that Philip wanted to appoint Perrenot as archbishop of Mechelen and primate of the Low Countries. Although Perrenot had not initiated the scheme, he had thwarted Orange's attempts to become governor of Brabant, and it thus appeared to William that Philip's principal adviser was determined to reduce the power of the nobility and abbots. When Perrenot became Cardinal Granvelle in 1561, he naturally became the focus of the growing discontent in the Netherlands (**62, 64**).

The onset of civil war in France in June 1562 provided the leading discontented grandees with the opportunity to put pressure on Philip to dismiss Granvelle. Philip wanted Margaret to dispatch troops to France to help the French king, Charles IX, who was faced with civil war. William of Orange persuaded Margaret that money, not men, should be sent and she allowed baron Montigny to travel to Spain to put the argument to Philip. While in Spain, Montigny realised that Philip's preoccupation with the Turks in the Mediterranean made it almost impossible for him to send money to the Netherlands. More significantly, it was also clear that Philip would not be able to send troops either. This fact emboldened the grandees to make a decisive attack on Granvelle.

On 11 March 1563, Orange, Egmont and Hornes informed Philip that they would resign if he did not dismiss Granvelle. To add force to their ultimatum Hornes organised the anti-Granvelle nobles into a league to show how much support they possessed. When it seemed that Philip might not accede to their demands, the States of Brabant decided to help by refusing to collect taxes. This act threatened to paralyse Margaret's administration and seriously undermined her authority. Margaret had never liked or trusted Granvelle and now she too decided to press for his dismissal.

Fortunately for Margaret, Granvelle's main supporter at Philip's court in Madrid, the duke of Alva, was not in attendance, and thus there was little to prevent Margaret's supporters from persuading the king to recall the cardinal. On 13 March 1564 Granvelle went into exile in Burgundy. On 30 July the Brussels government agreed to drop the incorporation plan in Brabant and promised to pay the new bishops a fixed stipend. The proposal for appointing ecclesiastical inquisitors was also dropped. In return the States of Brabant increased their payments to the government, and the nobles began to regain their monopoly of government business by working more closely with the regent in the Council of State. For most of 1564 affairs in the Netherlands began to get back to normal.

## The heresy factor – a turning point?

While Granvelle was in Brussels, Orange and the other dissident nobles had been careful to avoid directly blaming Philip for the new schemes in the Netherlands. They made it appear that Granvelle was the main butt of their criticisms. In practice this was not the case and Granvelle had warned Philip of Orange's deviousness and hypocrisy – elements of his character which earned William the misleading epithet 'the Silent' [**doc. 18** (i)]. Orange and the high nobility certainly aimed to further their own interests by seeking ways to limit the power of Philip and his regent. They wished to preserve their monopoly of senior posts in state and church and to reserve all important decisions to the Council of State, which they now dominated. Similarly most of the grandees were not initially concerned to make a stand against the persecution of heretics, and there was little understanding between the high nobility and the Protestant critics of Philip's policies. However, once Granvelle had been recalled, some of the nobility joined with the dissenting religious groups in criticising Philip's general religious policy in the Netherlands.

In a speech in the Council of State in December 1564, Orange expressed his disapproval of any prince who attempted to control the conscience of his subjects and he insisted on the need for major changes in Philip's religious policies. Orange was careful not to recommend armed rebellion, but his criticisms were made against a background of growing unrest in the Netherlands and the unspoken implication of his speech was that if nothing was done violence might get out of hand.

Between December 1563 and January 1565 there was a trade war with England which particularly affected Flemish textile workers and caused widespread unemployment. At the same time, a war involving Denmark, Sweden, Poland, Russia and the

Hanseatic towns of North Germany effectively closed the Baltic Sea to other European traders. The Netherlands had grown dependent on the Baltic trade for food (especially grain) and employment, and when that trade was dramatically cut back, the economy of the Low Countries suffered accordingly.

This unfavourable economic situation was exacerbated by poor weather. The winter of 1564–65 was bitterly cold and the harvest of 1565 was ruined. Bread became expensive and there were a number of food riots. Ominously, magistrates began to note how much of this unrest also involved the religious issue. After a riot in Ghent in August 1565, the local magistrates feared 'the evident danger from the dearth of corn and the large number of paupers, coupled with the arrival in this town of about 300 people from the region of Armentières who, it is to be feared, are infected with heresy'. In Brussels in the same year a government minister predicted that 'If the people rise up ... the religious issue will become involved'.

Charles V's persecution of heretics had been so successful that during his reign many Reformed communities were broken up and large areas were lost to the Protestant movement. Calvinism, as we have seen, came late to the Netherlands and there was no established Calvinist church there until 1555 or 1556. Nevertheless, after the massacre of Calvinists (Huguenots) by Catholics at Vassy in France in 1562, many French Calvinists took refuge in towns across the border in the southern Netherlands and formed 'churches under the cross' (in hiding). Calvinism began to spread rapidly after this, and the local Dutch magistrates tended to leave its supporters alone.

Although Charles V's heresy laws had made it a treasonable offence to hold heterodox opinions, local authorities had been offended by the way government inquisitors had been given the right to deal with heresy cases over their heads, and in retaliation magistrates refused to proceed against heretics if they were in other ways law-abiding. By 1564 there were few heresy trials or executions. Orange and Egmont, reflecting public opinion, argued that if the law was not being observed it ought to be changed and the penalties against heretics reduced. After William's speech in the Council of State the government allowed Egmont to travel to Spain to present this case to Philip in person.

Egmont remained in Spain until 6 April and returned to the Low Countries convinced that Philip had consented to a relaxation of the heresy laws and recognition of the supremacy of the Council of

State. Egmont encouraged the Council to set up a committee of theologians to consider how to modify the laws. He was in such high spirits that few Councillors were worried about the lack of a written statement of Philip's views. In fact Philip had told his secretary to give Egmont instructions which made it quite clear that the hard-line policy on heresy was to continue: 'Under no circumstances do I wish the punishment to stop: I only wish the method [of punishment] to be examined. And although it seems to me that Egmont wants the punishment to be mitigated, I do not wish this to be considered or interpreted in that way. Only the method is to be discussed' (**80**, p. 64) [**doc. 2**]. When letters arrived from Spain ordering the execution of six Anabaptists, Egmont was discredited.

Nevertheless the committee of theologians went ahead and recommended changes in the heresy laws, and the nobles felt confident that Philip would have to approve them. The Council of State calculated that the Turkish siege of Malta (March to September 1565) would keep Philip distracted from affairs in the Netherlands. However, by September the duke of Alva had regained influence at Philip's court at the expense of those who advocated compromise in the Netherlands. He was given the task of composing a series of letters to deal with all important issues relating to the government of the Netherlands.

The letters were drafted at Philip II's country house in the Segovia Woods and signed on 17 and 20 October 1565. They constituted an uncompromising restatement of Philip's plans for the Low Countries as of 1559 and totally rejected the suggested reforms of the committee of theologians and the plans to enhance the status of the Council of State. Rather than make concessions, Alva used the Segovia Woods letters to lay down an open challenge to the nobility in the Netherlands: they were to obey and enforce the heresy laws or be deemed guilty of treason.

# 3 The First Revolt, 1566–1568

## The 'Compromise of the Nobility'

Between 16 November and 20 December 1565 the Council of State considered the details of the Segovia Woods letters, and eventually called upon all provincial authorities to enforce the laws against heresy. However, many grandees and leading noblemen had met on a number of occasions during September and November to discuss political developments and now they considered resisting the king's orders. The lesser nobility were also intent on showing their hostility to the king's policies and the publication of the letters from the Segovia Woods strengthened their resolve. Under the direction of John Marnix about 400 lesser noblemen, including Brederode and Louis of Nassau, signed a document known as the 'Compromise of the Nobility', by which they agreed to confederate together to resist the inquisition. The grandees refused to sign the Compromise but they helped the confederates by refusing to enforce the heresy laws in their own provinces. William of Orange even asked Margaret to relieve him of his governorship on the grounds that he felt unable to enforce Philip's policies.

The confederates of the Compromise wanted to present the regent with a petition in the form of a 'Request' for changes in the laws. They met with Orange and other grandees to secure their support, but Egmont took fright and forewarned Margaret of their plans. This forced the confederates to go ahead alone, and on 5 April 1566 300 of them, led by Brederode and armed with guns, forced their way into Margaret's court and presented her with their 'Request' [**doc. 3**].

This open challenge to the government alarmed and angered Margaret and her ministers, one of whom described the confederates as *les Gueux*, 'the beggars'. The nobles made it quite clear that if Margaret rejected their petition, armed resistance was likely. Realising the vulnerability of her position, Margaret responded on 9 April by ordering the distribution of a document called the 'Moderation' which instructed all judges and magistrates not to enforce the heresy laws as harshly as Philip had ordered (although heretics were still not allowed to hold open meetings).

However, the Moderation did not fully satisfy the opposition at court. After all, Margaret had to secure the approval of Philip before the new instructions could be properly authorised and there was no guarantee that he would respond favourably. Yet Margaret was totally dependent on the support of the grandees for restraining the 'Beggars' and enforcing her 'Moderation'. They sought to exploit this dependency by forcing her to ask Philip to concede more favours to noblemen and to enhance the powers of the Council of State. Orange, Egmont and Hornes threatened to resign their posts and leave the Netherlands for Germany if Philip rejected their suggestions.

It was decided that Hornes's brother Floris, baron of Montigny, would travel to Spain with the Marquis of Berghes to secure Philip's ratification of the 'Moderation' and his approval for giving the Council of State supreme authority. While on his way to Spain, Montigny secretly visited his cousin, the constable of France, Anne de Montmorency, and discussed with him and other leading French Calvinists (Coligny, d'Anderlot and Châtillon) the possibility of securing help from the French Huguenots should there be armed resistance to Spain in the Netherlands. Once in Spain, the two envoys explained to Philip how the growing unease and disorder in the Netherlands had been caused by the king's religious policies and they encouraged him to give them a quick and favourable reply.

However, news of Montigny's meeting with the Huguenot leaders had been relayed to Philip and although at first he was reluctant to believe stories about military preparations in the Netherlands, he was keen to investigate them further before giving the envoys a response. Furthermore, he had been planning to visit the Netherlands in person and he did not want to preempt any future dealings with the Council of State. His thoughts were also distracted by the presence of yet another Turkish fleet off Italy.

Eventually, Montigny's persistence succeeded in forcing Philip to make a number of limited concessions. However, not long after these instructions were relayed to Brussels in the summer of 1566, news reached Philip that Margaret's control of the Low Countries had been undermined by the Beggars and Calvinists. On 22 September the Spanish royal council met in Madrid and decided that 'If the Netherlands situation is not remedied, it will bring about the loss of Spain and of all the rest' (**80**, p. 88). Philip then resolved to send an army to restore civil and religious order by force. What brought about this sudden deterioration in Spain's position in the Netherlands in the summer of 1566?


## The crisis of 1566–67: iconoclasm

Calvinist exiles began to ignore Margaret's prohibition of open meetings and to hold public services throughout the western Netherlands. These open air services attracted hundreds, sometimes thousands, of people, many of whom were armed. Not surprisingly, the local authorities were afraid to use force to break them up. From April 1566 the Calvinists made improvements in their organisation and asked Geneva to send more pastors and to arrange for more preaching in the Low Countries. By July 1566, it was clear that the grandees had lost control of the situation and they sought the help of the confederate Beggars to limit the meetings.

On 30 July, the confederates attempted to exploit this turn of events by forcing the grandees and Margaret to consider a second 'Request', even before Philip's response to the first one had been received in Brussels. Margaret was understandably angry, but persuaded the confederates to wait for twenty-four days in the expectation that by then a favourable reply to the first 'Request' would have arrived from Philip and that this might convince them of the need for moderation. In the meantime the Beggars agreed to keep the peace and to prevent the Calvinists holding more large open air services.

However, it soon became clear that the confederates had also lost control. Only the Calvinist pastors seemed to be in command, and they were intent on making more converts. Although the majority of these preachers had been born in the Netherlands, many of them were foreigners from Geneva, France, England and Germany. Their sermons were couched in inflammatory language and often incited audiences to smash images in local churches, convents and monasteries. Calvinists believed that man-made images of sacred subjects insulted God. They thought it was a sacred duty to remove idols from places of worship and that Protestants should only attend churches that had been duly 'purged' or 'cast down'. This iconoclasm, or image-breaking, had occurred earlier in Scotland and France and it did not originate in the Low Countries. However, in the circumstances of the Netherlands in

1566, iconoclasm constituted a greater threat to government control than would otherwise have been the case (**21**).

The effects of the trade war with England and the war in the Baltic combined with severe food shortages to create a very tense and chaotic situation which the Calvinist preachers exploited for their own ends (**69**, p. 288). In the southern provinces throughout August and September Catholic centres of worship were ransacked by an orderly and relatively small group of determined iconoclasts. In the north, there was more popular participation in the desecration which often took place in front of large crowds. Even so, there were few cases of more than 200 people being involved at any one time. Orange, Egmont and Hornes, who between them governed all the provinces of the western Netherlands, declined to act against the Calvinists. Many of the lesser nobility, such as Culemborg and Brederode, openly supported the image-breaking. Little wonder, then, that the magistrates, so recently instructed to show restraint in their dealings with heretics, should also have turned a blind eye to the destruction.

How much support did the iconoclasts have? Apart from Ghent, active support for the image-breaking seems to have been slight (**80**, p. 80). Yet it is clear that passive support was widespread. For many Netherlanders, Philip's policies had turned the Catholic Church into a mouthpiece of Spain, a threat both to traditional privileges and local independence, and there was much sympathy for the iconoclasts. However, the grandees and the majority of the nobles did not view the iconoclasts as anything more than temporary allies in the general resistance to Philip's religious policies. The disreputable activities of the image-breakers did not claim the lasting allegiance of many Netherlanders. Indeed, the grandees were, for a time, alarmed by the rapidity with which government authority collapsed.

On 31 July, Margaret received Philip's reply to the first 'Request', but decided not to publish it on the grounds that by then it would have appeared to offer too little too late. Instead, on 23 August the regent reluctantly granted the confederates their second 'Request': freedom of Protestant worship where it was already allowed (though not elsewhere). In return, the confederates signed an 'Accord' with the grandees promising to prevent further desecration and to keep the peace. The Accord was welcomed by many Netherlanders who had been frightened by the extremism inherent in some of the popular disturbances. However, it was an empty agreement. The confederates were now no more than a pale reflection of their original 'Compromise' group, and in recognition of this fact, just two days after signing the Accord, they dissolved their confederation. This did not bode well for Margaret's attempt to re-establish harmony in the Netherlands.

The Calvinists were not happy with the terms of the agreement of 23 August, and image-breaking continued. They sought to establish local compromises with the grandees to allow full Protestant worship (excluding only the Anabaptists\*) in any area. Orange arranged such a local Accord at Antwerp on 4 September. Hornes and Egmont did the same at Tournai (on the 7th) and Ghent (on the 8th). Not surprisingly, many similar compromises followed in Flanders, Brabant, and Holland.

Margaret was appalled at the prospect of unrestricted open Calvinist worship and she felt her three leading grandee advisers had let her down badly. In Orange's absence, Margaret persuaded the Council of State to denounce the Antwerp Accord and the other local compromises. During August and September, in this bitter frame of mind, the regent wrote Philip a number of letters in which she painted a black picture of the state of affairs in the Netherlands and advised him that there were just two lines of action open to him: to abandon the Low Countries altogether, or to send an army to restore order by force.

In fact the grandees were not as happy with the situation as Margaret imagined. Orange had only wanted Philip to grant freedom of conscience. He had not demanded that the Calvinists be given the right of public worship and he opposed the use of arms by the confederates. He sought a middle-of-the-road policy which would not alienate the Catholics and moderate nobility. He was not a supporter of the Calvinists and disliked the iconoclastic desecration [**doc. 18** (ii) and (iii)]. Egmont was similarly hostile to the Calvinists, and had a number of leaders of the disorders arrested and executed. The grandees were reluctant both to enforce the heresy laws too harshly or to do without them altogether.

In this uncertain atmosphere, the leading grandees met at Dendermonde on 3 October 1566 to appraise their situation. By then they were aware that Philip was very angry with them for not acting as guarantors of the second 'Request' and for not supporting Margaret's attempts to prevent the image-breaking. They knew he was planning to send an army to restore order and they felt like marked men. Some decided to fortify their family homes and to arm their households (**80**, p. 83). They were right to be worried, for Philip's other imperial problems temporarily abated and gave him the chance to concentrate on the Netherlands.

## The crisis of 1566–67: the Spanish debate and the defeat of the rebels

Philip was always loath to embark on a new policy without carefully debating the issues involved, and this often made decision-making a slow process. He inherited an elaborate network of interlinked councils whose main purpose was to amass, process, analyse and summarise information so that he, and he alone, could make informed decisions on all aspects of government. No single council was ever allowed to dominate him fully, and no individual or group (at least until the last few months of his life), ever came to dominate him completely. He relied on various sources for advice both from within and outside Spain, and he always reviewed his decisions in the light of changing circumstances and alternative policies. This can be seen in his handling of the debate on the Netherlands which began at the Escorial on 29 October 1566 (**64**).

Ruy Gómez, the prince of Eboli, wanted the king to go to the Netherlands in person, believing that Philip's presence would count for more than the actions of a large punitive army. He argued that the Netherlanders would accept the right concessions out of respect for the person of the king. Had not the king, he argued, always promised to return to the Netherlands?

Yet most advisers thought that the recent turn of events in the Netherlands made it unsafe for Philip to return there in 1566. The duke of Alva believed that the only course of action open to the king was a military one, using as many troops as were available. Philip also took advice from his correspondents in Italy and the Netherlands itself before accepting Alva's argument. He had been alarmed by the reports Margaret had sent him during the summer, and his correspondents in the Netherlands had suggested that the regent was so dependent on the grandees that she might well be forced to do their bidding. On 2 November he advised his chief engineer to arrange the necessary details for a military campaign, and on 29 November Philip appointed the sixty-year-old Alva commander of the army. Even so, changing circumstances and new arguments almost persuaded Philip to reverse his decision and cancel the expedition.

Initially, the events in the Netherlands between November 1566 and May 1567 seemed to confirm Margaret's assessment of the weakness of royal authority. News that Philip was sending an army to restore order caused great anxiety amongst those who had most to fear from reprisals. Some of the grandees and confederates considered raising troops to defend themselves and corresponded with relatives in Germany to that end. Although the leading grandees were unwilling to take the crucial step of raising troops themselves, some of the confederates were more resolute. Montigny had already established links with leading French Huguenots, but it was clear that the Calvinists and confederates were intent on taking more positive steps to defend themselves. Calvinist consistories raised money as part of a plan to bribe Philip II into granting toleration. If Philip rejected the plan, then the money was to be used to pay for troops recruited in Germany.

In November 1566, Margaret decided to garrison troops in some of the more restless or 'bad towns' (*villes mauvaises*) to forestall further trouble However, two of them, Tournai and Valenciennes, closed their ʁates to the troops. Margaret responded on 17 December by declaring the offending towns to be guilty of treason and rebellion. At the same time she laid siege to Valenciennes. She had asked the 'good towns' (*villes bonnes*) to suppress Calvinism, but this only provoked a hostile reaction from the Calvinists of the *Westwarter* of Flanders, who began to raise troops. Calvinist pastors ordered each consistory in West Flanders to raise one hundred men under the leadership of a captain. A central treasury was established and consistories made contributions to it. A relief force for Valenciennes was gathered at Tournai.

However, the Calvinists were poorly-trained and led and after one of their detachments had been defeated at Wattrelos on 28 December, the Calvinists at Tournai unwisely decided to attack the royalist troops at Valenciennes. They were easily defeated at Lannoy. Subsequently, on 2 January 1567 Tournai was forced to open its gates, surrender its arms and admit a garrison. Valenciennes held out until 24 March 1567. This was partly because the town's defences were difficult to break down, but also because Brederode, from his castle at Vianen, still posed a serious threat to Margaret.

Brederode had raised a number of infantry companies at Vianen and had been appointed leader of the Beggars (*Grands Gueux*), and official 'Protector' of the Calvinist movement. He drew up a third 'Request', and on 29 January 1567 met the grandees at Orange's home at Breda in an attempt to enlist their support. When they refused, Brederode went to Antwerp to seek an audience with

Margaret. She refused to see him. Feeling humiliated, Brederode reacted by raising more troops and establishing a special training camp for them at Oosterweel.

Brederode's militancy frightened the grandees and they now supported the government in its attempt to undermine the opposition. Egmont supplied Margaret with troops and routed the rebels at Oosterweel on 13 March. He then went to Valenciennes to direct the siege of the town. The town's last hope was that the French Huguenots would send a relieving army. When it became clear that no such help would materialise, Valenciennes surrendered and other 'bad towns' quickly followed its example. Even Antwerp accepted a garrison in April 1567. Brederode's castle fell on 3 May and Brederode himself deserted his troops and fled to Emden. William of Orange, discredited both at Philip's court in Spain and among the radicals in the Netherlands, and afraid for his life, resigned his offices on 10 April and eleven days later fled to Germany. By the middle of May 1567 the first serious crisis of royal authority in the Netherlands was over. Margaret wrote to Philip to suggest that his army was not needed after all. Armed resistance and open Calvinist worship were at an end. Why, then, did Philip persevere with his plan to send Alva and his army?

Montigny and Berghes were still in Spain, and they almost persuaded Philip that the best course of action was to send Ruy Gómez to the Netherlands with full powers as the king's personal representative. However, even as late as February 1567, Margaret was still sending Philip alarming reports about the activities of the rebels, and these seemed to underline the need for quick and dramatic action. Ironically, news from Margaret concerning the defeat of the rebels arrived in Madrid on the very day Alva left Spain for Italy.

Nevertheless, the King's Council again debated the arrangements for the Netherlands. It was clear that the main areas of disturbance had been Flanders and the southern Netherlands, and that the protests were mainly against Philip's system of government in religion and politics, not against foreign domination as such. The Eboli group once again argued that Philip had to regain the support of those who had been alienated by his policies, and that he could not afford to risk further trouble by sending an army. Certainly many Calvinists had supported the iconoclasm and some of the nobles close to Brederode had thrown themselves recklessly into armed opposition, but it was important to note how little positive support these groups had obtained and how easily they had been repressed. Although the king's advisers were evenly divided on the issue, Philip decided not to cancel the military expedition. He knew he had to deal with the problems of the Netherlands at some point, and, with news of the death of the Ottoman Sultan, Philip considered 1567 to be as good a time as any to send his troops northwards. Thus, on 18 June 1567, Alva finally set off with his army on the 700-mile land route from Lombardy to the Netherlands.

## Alva and the invasion of William of Orange

On 3 August, after an arduous march across the Alps and along the Rhine, Alva entered the Netherlands near Thionville. He reached Brussels on 22 August and took immediate steps to establish his authority. Margaret was to retain all executive civil power, and Alva was to prepare the ground for Philip to visit the Netherlands in the autumn. However, it soon became clear that Alva considered himself directly responsible to Philip II and that he was prepared to override the regent's authority when he thought it necessary. For instance, much to Margaret's annoyance, Alva billeted his troops in towns that had been loyal to her during the troubles. To the Netherlanders, the Spanish troops were insufferable, but Alva trusted them more than he did those raised by Margaret during 1566–67. Despite her objections, he summarily dismissed the regent's troops and, without informing Margaret, created a special judicial court – the 'Council of Troubles' – to try those accused of rebellion or heresy (**72**).

Alva had to keep the existence of the Council a secret because he wanted Margaret to lure the grandees back from Germany to Brussels, and he rightly supposed that she would not co-operate with him if by doing so she appeared to be his accomplice in their subsequent arrest and trial. Egmont, Hornes and von Stralen were arrested on arrival in Brussels, at which point Margaret realised she had been used and resigned her office (8 September 1567). On Philip's invitation. Alva succeeded her as Governor-General. Few Netherlanders missed the symbolism of the change: no longer was the Burgundian inheritance ruled by a prince of the blood.

Although Alva was not prepared for this role, he soon set about creating a new Spanish administration. Spanish and Italian ministers assumed executive power and only those native administrators were employed whom Alva considered to be reliable. He worked closely with a 'Cabinet Council' composed mostly of Spaniards which distributed tasks to other central government bodies. Spanish and Italian lawyers were employed to deal with foreign affairs, and to unify the many legal codes of the provinces. Alva believed that all the really important issues concerning the Netherlands had to be debated and dealt with in Madrid, for only men untainted with the corruptions of service in the provinces could make the necessary objective and disinterested decisions to maintain sound and effective government there. However, though he planned to employ a new team of Spanish administrators in the provinces when all the old local officials had either resigned or died, he was forced initially to depend on Netherlanders to administer his regime. Thus the infamous Council of Troubles, seen by many historians as the harsh instrument of Spanish rule in the Netherlands, was staffed mainly by existing administrators. They, in turn, followed up enquiries initiated largely by allegations made by local people to provincial tribunals which were similarly staffed principally by Netherlanders.

It angered Alva that William of Orange had not fallen into the same trap as Egmont and Hornes and returned to Brussels on Margaret's invitation. He tried to have Orange captured, but failed and had to be content with kidnapping his son, Prince William, who was a student at Leuven. Nevertheless, Alva pressed on with arresting, trying and executing home-based Netherlanders suspected of being involved in the troubles of 1566–67. Between 1567 and 1576 the Council of Troubles found nearly 9,000 persons guilty of complicity in the disturbances, of whom over 1,000 were executed. Those who escaped execution lost some or all of their goods. Most exiles, like Orange, were tried in their absence and judged to forfeit all their possessions and property. Even Montigny, who had remained in Spain to negotiate with Philip, did not escape, for he was held under house arrest and eventually, in October 1570, strangled on the King's orders.

With the death of Berghes (August 1567) and Brederode (February 1568) and the imprisonment of Egmont and Hornes (they were executed in June 1568), William of Orange became the undisputed leader of the opposition. However, it was clear that he, like all the other exiles, could only regain his lost authority and possessions if he invaded the Netherlands and overthrew Alva's new regime. He later claimed that Philip had forced him to take up arms and that he was not by nature a rebel. There is some truth in the claim, but it is also clear that this sense of injustice committed Orange to a lifelong struggle against 'Spanish tyranny'.

31

Although the promotion of his family interests was a major reason for Orange's grim determination to carry on fighting even when all seemed lost, it is also true that because the interests of the Nassau family were so widespread in the Netherlands, he could, with a certain amount of justice, claim to stand for the wider 'common cause' of the Netherlands (**102**). Thus, during the winter of 1567–68, since as a sovereign ruler of Orange he was entitled to make war on his enemies, he issued commissions to Count Louis of Nassau and others allowing them to raise troops. It was a move which indicated that the anti-Spanish aspect of the opposition had now come to the fore. Orange declared that Philip was bound by oath to respect the rights and privileges of 'our dear fatherland' and that if the king broke the conditions then the Netherlanders were no longer bound to obey him. In this way Orange argued that those who took up arms against Philip were not rebels. Rather they were 'liberators' who sought the deliverance of the 'fatherland' and to make the king keep his promises [**doc. 4**].

Orange planned to attack the Netherlands with four armies: French Huguenots from the south; a force from England into Flanders; troops from Germany into the south- and north-east; while he himself would command a reserve army based at Cleves. Nothing went right for Orange. One German army was defeated at Dalheim on 25 April. Count Louis's other German army was hemmed in at Delfzijl on the river Eems and attempted to use the sea lanes to England to get help from the churches-in-exile there. By this naval activity Louis's men gained the nickname 'Sea Beggars'. On 18 July a French Huguenot army was defeated at St Valéry by an army sent by the French king, Charles IX. On 21 July Alva smashed Count Louis's forces on the small peninsula at Jemmigen and many Orangists drowned in the river rather than be butchered by the Spaniards. Queen Elizabeth of England and German princes who had been contemplating helping Orange now withdrew their offers of help. Orange was left isolated and although he invaded with 30,000 men in October 1568, his troops were not used to fighting far from home and soon deserted him. After twenty-nine days of fruitless skirmishing, Orange was forced to retreat to France. Militarily, financially, and politically Orange's 1568 campaign had been a disaster. In 1569 he and his brothers had to content themselves with fighting for the French Huguenots under Coligny and Condé while Alva pressed on with establishing his regime in the Netherlands.

appearing. Orange was afraid that Netherlanders would accept Alva's advice, and he wrote from exile encouraging his supporters not to allow themselves 'to be further deceived by these totally false and vain promises which your oppressors and common enemies put about in order to win a richer booty later' (**63**) [**doc. 4**]. The anti-Spanish propaganda continued unabated.

Spanish soldiers were particularly criticised for their barbaric behaviour, and many of the propaganda flysheets and pamphlets painted lurid pictures of alleged excesses perpetrated by the troops. This propaganda campaign was as much an attempt to turn foreign opinion against Philip II and Alva as it was to give the Netherlanders resolve to resist the new regime. The fact that the propaganda often described excesses of Spanish troops indicates how keen the exiles were to undermine Alva's military superiority, for they knew that his legislative initiatives depended almost entirely on the existence of a large and expensive Spanish military establishment in the Netherlands. Indeed, the problem of financing this large military commitment began to trouble Alva himself.

Alva calculated that his total annual budget for defence was 1.87 million florins as compared with 2.3 million florins for adminis-tration. In 1568 Philip had raised the equivalent of £80,000 from Genoese bankers for shipment to Alva, but because of bad weather the ships had been forced to shelter in Plymouth and Elizabeth I had appropriated the money. Philip II could not afford to lose such amounts and he informed Alva that Spain could not supply him with any more money. Consequently, on 9 March 1569, Alva convened all the Estates of the Netherlands and asked their permission to collect three new taxes: the Tenth, Twentieth and Hundredth Pennies. The last of these was a single once-for-all tax of 1 per cent on all capital (the value of which was to be calculated at market prices). The Estates agreed to this tax and it was collected very efficiently (by being entrusted to central government inspectors and collectors and not to the normal tax 'farmers'). In all, the Hundredth Penny tax produced 3.6 million florins. However, the two other taxes aroused a great deal of opposition.

The Twentieth Penny tax was to be a 5 per cent levy on future sales of landed property and the Tenth Penny tax was to be a 10 per cent levy on all other sales. Alva hoped that these taxes would yield 13.6 million florins per annum, and intended that both taxes should be permanent. The estates rejected the schemes and offered instead to raise 4 million florins for Alva over a two-year period. The duke accepted this alternative plan, but looked upon it only as a temporary expedient. Although Alva made some concessions over the Tenth Penny, he continued to press forward with plans to implement the taxes. On 31 July 1571, when the Hundredth Penny revenue was running out, Alva declared his intention of collecting the new taxes even if the Estates objected. The result was a tax strike. When Alva threatened to use troops to enforce collection, the Estates of Artois, Flanders, Hainaut and Brabant sent deputies to Spain to protest to Philip II in person. Discontent mounted as industry and trade were badly affected and unemployment increased. At this crucial moment, on 1 April 1572, the Sea Beggars attacked and won control of the port of Brill in south Holland. The second revolt had begun.

## 1572: the Sea Beggars and William of Orange

As a result of the persecutions of the Council of Troubles, about 60,000 Netherlanders fled during the governorship of the duke of Alva, many to England (to Norwich in particular), as well as to Germany (**86**). Most fled to existing communities of exiles which strengthened these 'churches under the cross' and encouraged the development of a secret communications system to keep the groups in touch with each other. On 4 October 1571, Calvinists in the Netherlands held a 'national synod' (meeting) at Emden. The aim was to draw up articles for the organisation and discipline of the Reformed Church in the Netherlands and the 'provinces' of England and Germany. The result was a tightly-knit organisation which could be galvanised into effective action if threatened.

However, the Calvinist leaders at Emden made it clear that they did not seek an open break with Spain and they avoided making a public commitment to the political struggle against Alva. This disappointed William of Orange who, since 1568, had strengthened his ties with the Calvinists in the expectation that they might be important allies in any future invasion. In France, by contrast, the Huguenots at their national synod at La Rochelle resolved to support their political leader, Coligny, in his opposition to the Catholics. The Dutch Calvinists were only prepared to join their French counterparts in a 'Confession of Faith', not in open revolt. Nevertheless, ensuing events gradually forced the Dutch Calvinists to take up the sword in defence of their faith.

One result of the synod of Emden was to give the 'churches under the cross' a greater sense of solidarity and purpose. Several of these exiled communities supported the activities of the piratical

Sea Beggars in their attacks on Alva's shipping. However, William of Orange was not entirely happy with the way the Beggars attacked neutral as well as Spanish ships and he was annoyed that their indiscipline made it impossible for him to use their ships as a basis for a war fleet. The Sea Beggars also offended the Dutch Calvinists since their piracy harmed Dutch trade. The traders of Emden and the Hanseatic League complained to Queen Elizabeth I that the privateers operating out of her ports had gone too far.

Elizabeth was in a difficult position in her relations with the Beggars (**2; 105**, Ch. 11). Her foreign policy was based on two main aims: the avoidance of war with Spain, and the obstruction of French influence and expansion in the Netherlands. Between August 1568 and April 1572, the queen was painfully aware that her attitude towards the Beggars could seriously undermine either of these priorities. Despite Elizabeth's decision in December 1571 to expel De Spes, the Spanish ambassador, after revelations of his role in the Ridolfi plot*, it was her continued succour of the Sea Beggars which most annoyed Philip II. In February 1572, in order to reduce the tension between the two nations, Elizabeth felt compelled to take more active measures against the Beggars. She knew this would undermine her chances of securing a defensive alliance with the French, but talks on that issue had foundered temporarily and the queen decided to use the opportunity to appease Spain. Even so, it was clear to Elizabeth that she could neither safely embrace the Sea Beggars, nor wholly reject them. Her predicament was: how could the Beggars be *made* to go without recourse to hostilities?

She ordered her fleet to police the Narrow Seas more effectively, and, through her Privy Council, she made it clear to the Beggar leader – La Marck – that she expected the Beggars 'with as much speede as they mae . . . to depart, and to remayne noe longer upon those coastes'. She did not make an open proclamation of eviction because, as the ineffectiveness of previous ones had indicated, this would only have revealed her impotence in governing and controlling the Beggars. On 1 March 1572, Elizabeth instructed specially-appointed commissioners to make proclamations in Kent, Sussex, Southampton, and the Isle of Wight repeating what earlier proclamations had asserted, that piracy was a capital offence but adding that the offences of the Beggars were 'acts of war'. Thus, La Marck could be arrested, but not indicted as a rebel or pirate. However, although Elizabeth had stretched her powers and her administration to the limits in taking this action, Philip II was not impressed by her efforts, which he considered to be suspiciously imprecise. In fact, as Elizabeth hoped, La Marck escaped arrest by putting to sea, but his subsequent attack on the port of Brill on 1 April nearly initiated a state of affairs in the Netherlands which she had long been hoping to avoid.

Although there appears to have been some planning behind the Beggar assault on Brill, and Alva had been warned of a possible attack several months previously, the raid took everyone by surprise. Alva had fortified Flushing and Walcheren and was in the process of putting the Scheldt-Meuse area in a state of defence, but he had also been forced to counter a possible invasion by William of Orange by deploying more troops in the south and when the Beggars attacked, Brill was practically undefended. Philip II had also been distracted by a new Turkish offensive in the Mediterranean, and after his fleet defeated the Turks at Lepanto* (7 October 1571) the Spanish king planned to mount a massive operation against the Turks in 1572 to press home his advantage. Thus the Beggars captured Brill without a fight.

The Beggars were emboldened by their success and also took control of Flushing to create two bridgeheads from which, in the summer of 1572, they made inroads into Holland and Zealand and gained control of many more towns. The success of the Beggars was not entirely to Orange's liking. He was annoyed that La Marck had not informed him of his plans so that operations could be combined and directed. Orange had planned a co-ordinated invasion of the Netherlands by his own army from Germany, by Huguenot troops from France and by the Sea Beggars on coastal ports. When the Beggars captured Brill on 1 April, the other armies were not ready to move. Although a force under Louis of Nassau captured Mons (the capital of Hainaut) in May, and another army under Count van der Berg took Zutphen, Orange was not ready to invade, and the French king, Charles IX, had not yet made up his mind to start a war with Spain. It is true that the Orangists and Beggars rapidly gained control of the north-east and encouraged a large area of the Low Countries to rise in open revolt, yet Alva's main concern was the impending attack by the French, and he calculated that he could easily suppress the Beggars at a later stage. Indeed, events in France were potentially far more threatening for Alva.

Since the ending of the third Civil War in France (September 1570), Orange's brother, Louis of Nassau, and some Huguenot leaders, gained an increasing influence over the young king Charles IX, much to the dislike of the king's mother, Catherine de Medici. By the summer of 1572 the Huguenots had almost persuaded Charles IX to transfer hostilities to the Netherlands in support of Orange. Louis of Nassau suggested to Charles that in exchange for French help, France would be allowed to control much of the southern Netherlands and the coast of Flanders. However, Charles prevaricated, perhaps waiting for Elizabeth I to make a declaration of war against Spain in support of a joint Anglo-French enterprise in the Netherlands.

Nevertheless, in July, while not committing himself fully to a war with Spain, Charles allowed a French force of 6,000 men to be despatched northwards to relieve the rebel army in Mons. At the same time, Orange, thinking the French had decided to support him fully, marched into the Netherlands with 20,000 men. Catherine was aghast at the possible consequences for France and her fears were confirmed when the French were ambushed and routed at St Ghislain. News of this defeat forced Orange to wait at Roermond until the main French army invaded. It never did.

It could be argued that the capture of Brill by the Beggars not only forced Orange to act with too much haste, but that it also forced the French Huguenots to move too quickly, with the result that the defeat at St Ghislain made Charles IX reconsider the whole idea of intervention in the Netherlands against Spain. This in turn provided the occasion for a major shift in French domestic politics, to the detriment of both the Huguenots and Orange.

Catherine de Medici used the defeat to persuade Charles that a war with Spain was not in France's interests, and that the Huguenots, and in particular their leader Coligny, had gained too much influence at court for the good of the monarchy (**105**, Ch. 9). Other anti-Huguenot groups at the court, led by Henry duke of Anjou and the cardinal of Lorraine, persuaded the king to adopt a policy of 'elimination' by which Coligny and the Huguenot leaders were to be killed and the Huguenot movement repressed. On 23 and 24 August (St Bartholomew's Day), some 3,000 Huguenots in Paris (gathered for the wedding of the Huguenot Henry of Navarre and the king's sister), were massacred (**105**, Ch. 10). This event had enormous significance for Orange's plans. With Coligny dead and the Huguenots fighting for survival there was no hope of a French invasion in support of the Orangists and Beggars. Not surprisingly, Orange thought the massacre was a 'stunning blow', for with French help 'we would have had the better of the duke of Alva and we would have been able to dictate terms to him at our pleasure' (**80**, p. 138).

Before the massacre, Elizabeth I had been worried about the projected French invasion of the Netherlands. She concluded a defensive alliance with France at Blois in April 1572 in the hope that she could have more influence on French activities. Although she sent some English 'volunteers' to Flushing, this was more with the aim of denying the French control of such a strategic port than of opening hostilities with Spain. She warned Coligny that England would not tolerate French gains east of the Straits of Dover, and she even made secret offers of support to Spain in the event of a French invasion if Philip promised to restore the Netherlands to its pre-Alva state. In effect, Elizabeth hoped to dissuade France from supporting Orange's projected invasion and to persuade Spain to demilitarise the Netherlands. The massacre of St Bartholomew's Day ended for some time any threat of French intervention in the Netherlands and forced Spain to make an agreement with Elizabeth in 1573 in order to allow Philip the chance to combat Orangist resistance. Thus Elizabeth's aim to preserve England's independence of both Spain and France meant she could not give full support to Orange and the Beggars. Orange had also tried to attract the support of Sweden, Denmark and the Turks for his invasion in 1572, but these negotiations came to nothing and thus, after the death of Coligny, Orange was isolated.

Alva soon retook Mons, and Orange, whose army melted away through lack of pay, retreated northwards. Alva followed Orange with the aim of punishing the towns that had defected to the rebels. The fighting which followed often resulted in atrocities. The inhabitants of some of the towns, especially Zutphen, Haarlem, Mechelen and Naarden, were put to the sword. The Beggars, under the unruly leadership of La Marck, retaliated with cruel reprisals of their own, but were forced, like Orange himself, to take refuge in the watery wastes of Holland and Zealand. Orange thought the end was near. He wrote to his brother John: 'I am bent on going to Holland and Zealand, to maintain the cause there as far as that may be possible, having decided to make my grave there' (**102**, p. 19) [**doc. 5**].

After the surrender of Haarlem, the duke of Medina Celi, Alva's successor-designate, wrote to Philip II: 'Affairs here are now at the point where either they will be brought to a speedy conclusion or else they will drag on for a very long time. Everything depends . . . on the decision to be taken on how to proceed in Holland, because there are many towns there to be forced into submission' (**80**, p. 160). Alva continued to support a military solution and disliked Medina Celi's growing opposition to the struggle. Philip II feared Alva's successes would be undermined by Medina Celi and he decided to replace Alva with the stern governor of Lombardy, Don Louis de Requesens. On 17 November 1573 the new governor entered Brussels and on 29 November he was sworn in as Alva's successor.

However, Requesens was forced at first to rely on the advice of Alva, and in a letter to his successor the old duke once again emphasised the need for a military solution: 'These troubles must be ended by force of arms without any use of pardon, mildness, negotiations or talks until everything has been flattened. That will be the time for negotiation'. Thus, throughout the governorship of Requesens (1573–76), Holland and Zealand were forced to organise themselves to fight an exhaustive defensive war (**67, 68**).

## Holland and Zealand

At first Orange's position was not strong. He had to make many compromises, and in 1573 he even became a Calvinist with the aim of securing further support. He knew that if the rebellion was not to be crushed by the first Spanish attack, Holland and Zealand had to accept three points: the need for a provisional government with the constitutional position of each participant clearly defined; a financial organisation to support the military action; and a religious policy which would attract widespread support. Orange presented these propositions to the States of Holland at a meeting in Dordrecht (Dort) in July 1572, and they were approved [**doc. 10**]. By this agreement the States recognised Orange as Governor-General and Stadholder of Holland, Zealand, Friesland and Utrecht, though nothing was said to undermine Philip II's formal supremacy. The new order was a contractual one, with power shared between Orange and the States. Orange promised to restore in full the rights and liberties of the States and to protect them 'from foreign tyrants and oppressors' (**63**, p. 54).

Initially, Zealand found it difficult to make the necessary changes, but she managed it in March 1574 and then followed this by signing an act of union with Holland on 4 June 1575. Orange was appointed to serve as chief executive of the new organisation. This represented a significant break with Spain, and in October the States made this explicit by declaring their wish to 'forsake the king and seek foreign assistance'. It soon became clear that such assistance was not immediately forthcoming and this prompted the provinces to sign a new defensive pact on 25 April 1576, by which the burdens of taxation were apportioned fairly and, until such time as some external person or body could be found, Orange was given sovereign authority. However, the Stadholder had to issue decrees in the name of 'His Excellency and the Estates' to mark the fact that power within the new republic was still to be shared with the traditional political rulers from the towns.

Although the new system did not effect a radical change in political relationships between the various social groups in Holland and Zealand, it did bring Orange the support of most of the lower-middle classes organised in the militias and guilds, and this in turn allowed him to lessen the opposition to Calvinism. Nevertheless, the new order was still faced with a number of potentially damaging problems.

In the first instance the new government system did not have the full support of all influential citizens, many of whom remained loyal to the old order and did not want to break with Philip II. There was also the danger of disillusionment and disunity amongst Orange's supporters if the changes failed to work. The defence of the provinces placed a heavy burden on the entire population and many people complained that taxation was far higher than it had been under Alva. This in turn encouraged a resurgence of particularism which not only threatened to set Holland and Zealand against each other, but to divide the north of Holland from the south and also, within these areas, to set one town against another. Orange managed to keep these tensions within manageable proportions not only through the strength of his personality, but also by propagandising the legend that he was the indispensable mediator, the Father of the Fatherland who was prepared to sacrifice his life and possessions for the sake of liberating the Netherlands from Philip II's military enslavement.

However, the area in revolt against Spain did not even include all of Holland and Zealand. Indeed, Amsterdam remained loyal to Spain, as did the greater part of Zealand. Furthermore, the area in revolt was soon reduced in size: in July 1573 the Spaniards captured Haarlem, and in June 1576 Zierikzee surrendered. It was fortunate for Orange, therefore, that the geography of the area allowed the rebels to defend themselves by large-scale flooding and sound defensive siege tactics based on the Italian idea of the bastion fortification (see Chapter 10). The four great rivers, the Lek, Linge, Maas and Waal, all reached the sea at the same delta and in the sixteenth century it was very difficult for an army to cross them from the south. By defending key towns at the most westerly crossings, Orange often forced the Spanish armies to march far inland before they could make a significant attack. Thus, although Orange's armed forces were only an amalgam of Beggars, foreign volunteers and native levies, their task was easier than that facing the Spanish *tercios*.

## Spanish mutiny and bankruptcy

Despite the adverse geographical conditions, the Spaniards re-took Naarden (1572) and Haarlem (1573), and on 22 April 1573 Brill was also recaptured. Although Philip suspended the hated Tenth Penny tax on 26 June he rejected every attempt to negotiate a compromise with the rebels, even though Alva was totally dependent on subsidies from Spain. This difficult financial situation spelled disaster for the army of Flanders which had been starved of resources and had often been restless to the point of open disobedience and mutiny. Alva pleaded with Philip to abandon the Spanish offensive against the Turks in the Mediterranean and to send more money to the Netherlands. However, a number of military failures, culminating in the loss of the royal fleet on the Zuider Zee in October 1573, persuaded Philip that Alva's aggressive policy was no longer working and was, on the contrary, proving too costly. Yet Alva's successor, Requesens, followed Alva's advice and continued to fight.

Further military failures at the beginning of 1574 (the fall of Middelburg, and the failure to take Leiden) made Spanish troops so restless that even the defeat of Louis of Nassau at Mook in April did not prevent the army from mutinying and holding Antwerp to ransom until its arrears of pay had been extracted. Even then the unrest in the army did not subside. Troops in other parts of Holland mutinied in late 1574 leaving their garrisons vacant for Orangists to occupy. Requesens, reflecting on these mutinies, thought that God was punishing Spain for some reason. He convinced himself that Spain's cause had lost divine support and that as a consequence, no amount of extra money from Madrid would bring the victory Philip sought. On 10 October 1574 he warned Philip: 'There would not be time or money enough in the world to reduce by force the twenty-four towns which have rebelled in Holland, if we are to spend as long in reducing each one of them as we have taken over similar ones so far' (**80**, p. 165; **79**).

Philip agreed with Requesens that Spain could ill-afford to keep on fighting in the Netherlands. In 1574 the running costs of the army of Flanders (86,000 strong) were estimated to be 1.2 million florins a month, which was more than the king's income from the Indies and Castile combined. Philip began to think that the Netherlands would be lost through lack of money. His financial advisers certainly wanted the king to abandon the war in the Netherlands and argued further that he had no option but to repudiate all his public debts. Philip feared this financial crisis would be exploited by his enemies: 'We are in great need and our enemies know it well, so that they will not wish to make a settlement'. In September, to confirm his fears, the Turks, possibly as a consequence of Orange's diplomacy, captured Tunis and the important fortress of La Goletta. In November Philip asked Requesens to begin peace negotiations with Orange and a conference was held at Breda in March 1575. Three months later, however, the talks broke up without agreement.

Orange had been prepared to recognise Philip's authority, if in return the king recognised Calvinism and accepted constitutional guarantees that those who had taken up arms would not be punished and that Spanish troops would be withdrawn. However, Philip was not prepared to make concessions on religious toleration despite his parlous financial state. When the talks broke up Orange and the States of Holland renounced their allegiance to Philip and offered the position of sovereign to Elizabeth I and then to the duke of Anjou. Both declined the honour and the new rebel regime was left to fight on alone.

Requesens reverted once more to using force and his troops, now more settled, pushed the rebels into the town of Zierikzee and laid siege to it. The town was strategically very important and Requesens calculated that by taking it he would cut the rebel provinces in two. However, when Zierikzee eventually fell in July 1576, the situation had changed. In September 1575 Philip had been forced to suspend interest payments on the Castilian public debt and this had placed Requesens in an impossible position. The decree of bankruptcy broke the governor's health and he died on 5 March 1576.

The death of Requesens clearly took Philip by surprise, since he did not immediately know who to appoint as his successor. The nine ageing members of the Council of State decided to govern by themselves. They were ill-equipped to do so, however, and royal authority, both civil and military, was soon on the verge of collapse. As a result of the bankruptcy Spanish troops in the Netherlands were once more deprived of pay, and instead of pressing home their advantage after the fall of Zierikzee, they mutinied. Although there had been mutinies of Spanish troops in the army of Flanders in previous years (1573, 1574, 1575), the mutiny of 1576 caused a hiatus in Spanish-Netherlands relations and transformed many previously moderate Catholics into potential rebels.

## The Pacification of Ghent and the widening of resistance

The Spanish mutineers of 1576 terrorised the local population, beggared the treasury and undermined all offensive action against the rebels. In this way the Spanish regime in the Netherlands was discredited and the provinces began to consider joint military action to defend themselves. Such a move was hastened by the action of the mutineers on 25 July when, in an unprovoked attack, they sacked the loyal town of Aalst just west of Brussels. As a result the States of Hainaut sought permission from the Council of State to open negotiations with the States of Brabant about common defence. The Council, under orders from Philip, refused to allow such a meeting. However, on 4 September, troops from the States of Brabant, fearing the situation would get worse if nothing was done, arrested the members of the Council of State. This event indicated that there were many Catholics who were prepared to use force to put an end to the disturbances, and some of the more radical of these sought to exploit the situation to pursue a more hostile anti-Spanish policy.

The duke of Aerschot, himself a council member and head of the powerful house of Croy, led the anti-Spanish Catholic nobility in the southern Netherlands. He was supported by his Croy relatives (such as the count of Roeulx, governor of Flanders), and also lesser Walloon nobility (like baron Champagney) who wanted the Spanish troops to be expelled and their ancient rights restored. There were also more radical groups (like the 'patriots') who were even more vehemently anti-Spanish and set up a number of revolutionary committees in towns in Flanders and Brabant. It was this rather unstable combination of anti-Spanish Catholics that, in September, engineered the summoning of a States-General of all provinces except Holland and Zealand to Brussels. The aim was to arrange for their mutual defence. Letters were also sent to King

Henry III of France and his brother, the duke of Alençon, requesting military assistance if needed. More significantly, some members of the States wrote to Orange for help in bringing the war to an end.

Despite the continued unease of some Catholic delegates, talks between Orange and the States, based on issues raised at Breda, began at Ghent on 7 October. An agreement was reached on 30 October. According to this, the fighting between the rebels and the other provinces was to end so that rebel and obedient provinces could combine their efforts to expel Spanish and other foreign troops from the Netherlands; Orange was recognised in all his offices; the religious *status quo* in all provinces was to be maintained and the heresy laws were suspended; all affairs of the Netherlands were to be referred to the States-General for settlement. Once the Spaniards had been expelled, a full States-General was to decide on a new political and religious organisation for the Netherlands.

Many Catholics were astonished at the speed with which the agreement was reached, but there appeared to be good reasons for haste. To succeed Requesens, Philip II had appointed his only brother, Don John of Austria, a champion of Catholicism and the victor of Lepanto*. By this appointment the deputies of the States-General assumed that Philip wanted the repressive Spanish policies to continue. As it turned out, they were right, but in the short term Philip II faced mounting pressure from the Turks in the Mediterranean, and the declaration of bankruptcy had forced him to send Don John to the Netherlands with instructions to make temporary concessions. Orange knew that there were those in the States-General who were likely to be duped by these concessions into accepting Don John's authority without, in return, forcing important guarantees from the king's new agent. Orange therefore sought to keep the details of the concessions secret while at the same time preserving the general anti-Spanish attitude of the States-General.

Fortunately for him, on 4 November, while the delegates were seeking ratification of the Ghent agreement (and the day after Don John had arrived in Luxembourg), Spanish forces attacked and cruelly sacked Antwerp. The 'Spanish Fury' in Antwerp lasted several days and 8,000 people lost their lives. As a result the agreement was quickly ratified as the 'Pacification of Ghent' and published on 8 November. Although it formally marked the end of the second revolt, the Pacification of Ghent certainly created the opportunity for Orange to unite the Netherlands against Spain (**5**).

# 5 From Fragile Unity to Deepening Crisis: the Break-up of the Netherlands, 1576–1584

The Pacification of Ghent, as we have seen, demanded the expulsion of Spanish and other foreign troops from the Netherlands; recognised William of Orange in all his offices; maintained the religious *status quo* in all provinces and the suspension of the heresy laws; and, most significantly, provided for the States-General to be the central organ of government. From 1576, the States-General could legislate, determine the times and frequency of meetings, negotiate with foreign powers (which included the exchange of ambassadors), conclude treaties, declare war and peace, and raise finances to pay for an army. It might be expected, therefore, that this institution was radically different in nature from its predecessors. This was not the case.

Despite an increase in the number of provinces represented (only Limburg, Luxembourg and Groningen refused to send representatives in order to avoid making extra financial commitments), and despite a corresponding increase in the numbers of delegates, the social composition of the assembly remained more or less the same, with noblemen, clergymen and town magistrates monopolising places. There was no sudden radicalisation of the States-General. The cumbersome and time-consuming decision-making process militated against fundamental change. Furthermore, although the the new States-General was not legitimately convoked by the king, this proved the basis for worry and anxiety rather than revolutionary fervour, and this unease, when combined with a general confusion about aims and direction, soon allowed old internal divisions and differences to reassert themselves.

The high nobility of the southern Netherlands, although hostile to centralisation and absolutism, still felt bound to the Habsburg dynasty. They were jealous of Orange's pre-eminence and mistrusted the prince's pursuance of a national ideal. They were moderate Catholics, who were just as appalled by the insurrectionary spirit of the Calvinists of the northern provinces as they were by the 'furies' of the Spanish troops. This potential for disunity was aggravated by the strength of provincial particularism and the continued threat of religious conflict. Thus, the first major decision that the States-General had to take – how to deal with Don John of Austria – led to a polarisation of opinion. Some representatives wanted to accept the duke unconditionally; others wanted to reject his authority outright; and a middle group wanted to negotiate.

Initially, the States-General refused to accept Don John unless he recognised the Pacification of Ghent and agreed to the withdrawal of Spanish troops. A ceasefire was concluded on 15 December and on 27 January 1577 Don John agreed to the States' demands in the 'Perpetual Edict'. The States in return promised to uphold the Catholic religion and to accept the authority of Don John as Governor-General. They allowed Don John to call a new States-General, but it had to be 'in the form it had when the Emperor Charles abdicated'. Thus, after Spanish troops finally left the Netherlands on 28 April, the States allowed Don John to be sworn in as Governor-General (1 May).

William of Orange had opposed any move to settle with Don John. He thought Philip II could not be trusted and that the concessions embodied in the Perpetual Edict would soon be ignored. William knew that the king had given way because he had no choice. He reasoned that as soon as Philip's financial position improved and the Turkish threat abated, the king would order Don John to reimpose royal authority in the Netherlands and disregard the humiliating settlement.

To show his annoyance at the compliance of the States-General, Orange boycotted the assembly. Don John tried to placate him, knowing that as long as Orange held aloof the states of Holland and Zealand would remain alienated from his government. Formal talks took place between Don John and Orange at St Geertruidenberg in an attempt to break the deadlock. However, it was clear that the rebel provinces were not prepared to sacrifice their reformed religion to satisfy the Edict. On 24 July, frustrated by the intransigence of Orange and his supporters, Don John seized the citadel of Namur as part of a plan to crush the States-General and impose his authority. When he failed to take Antwerp on 1 August, Don John was forced to recall the Spanish troops. It was now clear to all that the Governor-General could not be trusted and that Orange had been right all along. Deputies from Holland and Zealand once again took their places in the States-General. Nevertheless, despite the fact that Orange was held in high esteem once more, it was clear that the high nobility of the southern provinces, led by Aerschot, were still not prepared to see the prince dominate the States-General. They sought outside help.

At the instigation of Aerschot, the States-General arranged for Archduke Matthias (son of the Habsburg Emperor Maximilian II and nephew of Philip II), to replace Don John as Governor-General. It also sought help from France and England. Orange now realised that he would never have the full support of the States-General and that he would always have opponents who would question his authority, but this merely encouraged him to strengthen his position in the assembly. Ever since Granvelle had attained power in the Netherlands, Orange had coveted the post of *ruwaard* or governor of Brabant, and he now sought to be elected to this powerful position, calculating that he would then be able to dominate the new Governor-General. He knew that the patricians of the States of Brabant would oppose such a move and he began to use the support he had built up amongst the guildsmen of Brussels and Ghent to put pressure on the delegates. On 18 October a crowd of Orange's supporters marched into the chamber where the States of Brabant were meeting and forced the delegates to appoint Orange *ruwaard* until Matthias arrived.

For the duke of Aerschot (himself governor of Flanders) and other Catholic moderates the appointment of Orange, a Protestant, to high office was deplorable. For them, Orange represented a dangerous element of social and religious radicalism which threatened the authority of the grandees. Many of the Catholic grandees believed that they alone should administer the Netherlands and that the recent attempts by Orange and others to advance the authority of the States-General were fraught with danger. Thus, as a first step to curbing the authority of the national assembly, these Catholic grandees sought to limit the influence of Orange by securing more authority for Matthias.

Aerschot and his supporters were further alarmed by the events of 1576–77. In a number of towns in Brussels and Ghent guildsmen had been increasing their influence in municipal government and public affairs. Through their representatives (in Brussels they were known as 'the Eighteen'), the guildsmen had allowed Calvinist exiles to foment anti-Catholic unrest and make converts. In Ghent the guildsmen removed the provincial government, raised an essentially working-class militia and set up a special committee – also known as 'the Eighteen' – to control military affairs. The duke of Aerschot was even temporarily arrested. In 1578 neighbouring Oudenarde overthrew its council in a similar manner and the Catholic faith was banned. Other towns in Flanders, Brabant and Artois experienced the same process. Orange did not encourage the iconoclasm that often accompanied such activities, because Calvinist aggression undermined the Pacification of Ghent. Nevertheless these developments strengthened William's position in the States-General, and allowed him to persuade the deputies to impose restrictions on Matthias.

Much to the annoyance of Aerschot, Matthias was forced to seek the advice of a specially appointed council, approved by the States-General, before submitting his fiscal, legal and political policies to the Assembly for its consideration. More disturbing, from Aerschot's point of view, was the fact that Matthias also undertook to defend Holland and Zealand from any Spanish attack. Clearly, Orange had succeeded in establishing the States-General at the centre of the new political system in the Netherlands. He now sought to make himself the most powerful member within it. On 8 January 1578, he succeeded in persuading the States-General to make his appointment as *ruwaard* of Brabant a permanent one, which meant that when Matthias was sworn in on 20 January, Orange was his deputy and chief adviser, the *de facto* ruler of the country. Aerschot's first attempt to curb Orange's influence had failed (**110**).

## The Unions of Arras and Utrecht

On 18 August 1577 a fleet of ships from Peru arrived at Seville carrying more than 2 million ducats in bullion for Philip II. The king immediately negotiated a loan with his bankers in order to finance a new military offensive in the Netherlands. At the same time, peace with the Sultan meant that Philip could order his troops back into action and, under the leadership of Alexander Farnese, the prince (and later duke) of Parma, he soon had a string of victories to celebrate. On 31 January 1578 the army of the States was defeated at Gembloux. On 13 February, Leuven was taken. Orange, Matthias and the whole States-General fled to Antwerp. However, Aerschot and the grandees attempted to exploit this reverse for their own ends.

The Catholic deputies of the States-General had already appealed for help to Francis, duke of Alençon (brother and heir to the king of France). Not only was Alençon a prince of the blood, he also offered Aerschot and the grandees a second opportunity to create a 'third force' in the politics of the Netherlands to counter

Orange's power in the States-General. On 10 July 1578, Alençon, now duke of Anjou, entered Mons. Orange was not convinced that Anjou's intervention would solve any problems and he knew that the Catholic deputies were hoping to use Anjou's presence to undermine his own position. He therefore decided to use the duke for his own ends. On 13 August Orange persuaded the States-General to recognise Anjou as 'Defender of the Liberties of the Low Countries', but not to give him any share in government. Anjou's role was clear but restricted: to provide 12,000 men to fight against Parma's army (**50**).

However, the Catholic grandees had also sought help from England, and although Elizabeth I had been careful not to get involved in the war, she realised that Anjou's intervention necessitated an increased English presence in the Netherlands. Elizabeth encouraged John Casimir, the administrator of the Rhine Palatinate, to raise a mercenary army and lead it into Brabant, which he duly did on 26 August 1578. Orange was pleased that Elizabeth had responded so positively to Anjou's intervention, since Casimir's presence was seen by the prince as a precursor of further and more substantial English intervention against Spain, and also as a potential counterweight to any move by the Catholic grandees to exploit Anjou's initiative for their own political ends.

John Casimir proved more interested in furthering the Calvinist cause in Ghent than he did in engaging the Spaniards in battle, and the anti-Catholic activities of his men added impetus to the Calvinist conquest first of Haarlem and Amsterdam and then of the provinces of Utrecht and Gelderland. In the face of Spain's renewed efforts to impose royal authority and the Catholic faith, and the cumulative effects of Calvinist extremism and urban insurrection, the fragile unity of the Pacification of Ghent broke down.

It soon became clear that the States-General could not afford to pay so many troops. In September complaints about arrears of pay led to mutinies by Walloon 'Malcontents' in the army of the States-General. At this time the Walloon States were meeting at Arras to discuss the formation of a Catholic Union and the Malcontents joined them. The population of nearby Ghent feared that the Catholic forces would move against the city to reimpose Catholicism and they asked John Casimir for help. On 10 October fighting broke out between the two sides. It could not have started at a more inopportune time for the States-General.

Don John had died of the plague on 1 October and had been replaced as Governor-General by Parma. He had been Don John's aide since 1577 and, once confirmed as his successor, Parma soon displayed all the diplomatic and military skills required to transform a situation of near-defeat into one of Spanish reconquest (**34**). The fighting between Catholics and Calvinists allowed Parma to avoid defeat at Bouge and, more significantly, intensified all the old divisions between the seventeen provinces. The States-General was on the verge of collapse.

In the south, by the autumn of 1578, Flanders, Hainaut and Artois had refused to make further contributions to the war effort against Spain. In the north, Holland and Zealand had never acknowledged the authority of Don John and, from 1575, had attempted to form a special defensive confederation of provinces (a state-within-a-state). In January 1579, at the instigation of Gelderland, deputies from Holland, Zealand, Utrecht, Friesland, Gelderland and Ommelanden (near Groningen), met in Utrecht to conclude an act of alliance and union. By this union, the signatory provinces, referred to as 'United Provinces', were to act in perpetuity 'as if they were a single province' in matters of war and peace. In other matters and especially in religion, particularism prevailed and each province retained the right to govern itself in its own manner. The new confederation made no adequate provision for central institutions and it continued to send deputies to the States-General, but it did appoint a council, a treasurer, and a 'director' – John of Nassau.

The formation of the Union of Utrecht, in endorsing the spirit of the rebels of 1572, marked the end of the Pacification of Ghent. Orange was unsure about the move. For four months he refrained from joining the Union. In 1578 he had supported an attempt to pass legislation securing religious peace. By this programme, freedom of worship was to be guaranteed to Protestant and Catholic minorities where one hundred or more families so desired. This tolerant attitude had brought him opposition from the Calvinists in Ghent who labelled him an atheist. It was clear to him that such groups would not abide by the pious but empty toleration clauses of the Union. He had also been dismayed by the way that the States of Holland and Zealand had entered the Union negotiations without fully consulting him and with scant regard for the authority of the central government and the general struggle against Spain. Thus Orange was not surprised that the Union of Utrecht proved unacceptable to the Catholic majority in the States-General, or that it strengthened moves already afoot to establish a Catholic Union.

On 6 January 1579, this latter event came about when the States of Hainaut and Artois concluded a Union at Arras. They were soon joined by Walloon Flanders. Together these confederated provinces opened talks with Parma in February. On 6 April they were reconciled to Philip II by the Treaty of Mont St Eloi and offered their military support in the fight against the United Provinces. A formal peace was signed in Arras on 17 May (the Treaty of Arras) [**doc. 11**]. Thus, the Walloon provinces now joined Namur, Luxembourg and Limburg (who were already controlled by Spain) to become the 'obedient' provinces. In return Parma ratified their rights and privileges, confirmed both the Pacification of Ghent and the Perpetual Edict, promised to remove all foreigners from important posts and even agreed to withdraw his troops from the territory of the signatory provinces. In fact it took Parma some time, and not a little humour and bribery, to make the Walloon nobility feel secure in their titles and privileges. However, by 1582 he had gained their confidence to such an extent that they agreed to allow Spanish troops to return.

By May 1579, Orange had realised that he had to sign the Union of Utrecht if he was not to be isolated. Both Anjou and Casimir had returned home and the States-General was little more than a disorganised meeting place of deputies from disunited provinces. There seemed nothing to prevent Parma reconquering whole areas of the Netherlands and Orange needed the protection of the United Provinces.

There were still those in the States-General who imagined that a peaceful settlement could be negotiated to preserve the unity of the Netherlands, and they welcomed an invitation from Rudolf II, the Holy Roman Emperor, to attend another peace conference in Cologne in May 1579. However, Parma continued hostilities in the Netherlands knowing that it would be impossible to arrange a peace with Orange and the Calvinists, and he captured Maastricht on 29 June. This success emboldened the Catholic delegates in Cologne and they demanded the restoration of exclusive Catholic worship in all provinces, and fewer checks on Philip II's authority. Cardinal Granvelle became Philip's chief minister in Madrid on 1 August and he pressed a hard-line policy on the king, sensing that more towns would defect to the royalist cause. Mechelen fell to Parma on 27 July and in December Catholics in 's Hertogenbosch and Groningen prevented the Calvinists from gaining control (**26**). The peace talks at Cologne broke up in failure. There was no longer a middle way to peace and unity.

## Anjou and the Act of Abjuration

In March 1580, Philip II outlawed William of Orange, declaring him to be a traitor. Orange responded with his famous *Apology* which was presented to the States-General at Delft in December 1580. It was a personal defence of his role in Netherlands affairs and a justification of the activities of the rebel provinces. In it, Orange charged Philip II with being a murderer and a tyrant. He concluded that the States had the right to resist the king of Spain and his agents in the Netherlands (**109**). This personal statement seemed to persuade the united provinces that they had to make an open break with Philip II. Yet this raised the problem of who should replace the king.

Matthias was not considered suitable (though he did not resign until March 1581). The only real alternative seemed to be Anjou, especially since his leadership offered the States-General the hope that Henry III might declare war against Spain [**doc. 15**]. However, Orange had to negotiate long and hard with the States of Holland and Zealand to get them to agree even to discuss the terms of the conditions that should be placed on Anjou, so fearful were they of being ruled by a Catholic. An agreement between Anjou and the States-General was signed in September 1580 (the Treaty of Plessis-lès-Tours) [**doc. 12**]. On 23 January 1581, Anjou became 'prince and lord of the Netherlands' – but at a price. He was obliged to pledge the States-General and the provinces to maintain all their privileges, rights, and liberties. He was to call the States-General annually, although it could meet more regularly if it so decided. Anjou's Council of State was to be chosen by the provinces, who also provided him with the list of names from which he had to choose provincial governors. The very name of 'sovereign' was excluded from Anjou's list of titles because it smacked too much of absolute power. It was not a good beginning, and Catherine de Medici had already written to Anjou making known her anxieties about the dangers inherent in the situation and voicing her opposition to a possible war with Spain [**doc. 16**].

Yet, with the question of the succession settled, the States began to consider the mechanics of deposing Philip II. A 'Placard' was drawn up declaring that Philip was no longer sovereign and it was published on 26 July 1581 as the 'Act of Abjuration'. It was adopted by the deputies of Brabant, Gelderland, Zutphen, Flanders, Holland, Zealand, Utrecht, Friesland, Overijssel and Mechelen. Princes, it declared, were made for subjects, not subjects for

53

princes. It stressed that in the Netherlands the prince's power had always been conditional and based on agreements with the people to rule in conformity with ancient rights and liberties. Philip II was charged with violating these conditions and thus, the Act concluded, 'the king of Spain has by right forfeited his lordship, jurisdiction and inheritance of these provinces' [**doc. 13**].

The Act of Abjuration attempted to employ the theories found in the great Huguenot treatise, the *Vindiciae contra Tyrannos*, which had been written after the Massacre of St Bartholomew to justify resistance to a lawfully elected and ordained leader. In effect it was a declaration of independence, but it was made by a weak institution all too well aware of the general apathy and antipathy of most of the people of the Netherlands. There was also much confusion about where real sovereignty was to lie (see Chapter 11).

The Catholic 'obedient' provinces countered the defiant claims of the United Provinces with a flood of pamphlets and polemics. Even within the lands controlled by the rebel States there was opposition: from Catholics who still constituted the majority in most areas; from Anabaptists* who were against the swearing of oaths; from Lutherans who were anxious about the legality of resisting a properly ordained authority. Even some Calvinists found it difficult to take the new oath, especially office-holders and lawyers (**52**).

Clearly, the United Provinces needed outside help. Orange imagined that Anjou would be the saviour of the Netherlands. He was apparently engaged in an on-off courtship with Elizabeth I, and Orange might be forgiven for supposing that an Anglo-French union would be the answer to his problems. It is highly unlikely, however, that Elizabeth had any serious intention of marrying Anjou (her 'dear frog'). She used the bait of marriage to encourage Anjou to commit himself to the States-General at a time when the revolt seemed on the verge of collapse, and Parma's reconquest was threatening the delicate balance of power that Elizabeth sought to maintain in the Netherlands. Nevertheless, she did provide Anjou with money, about one-fourth of her regular income, which, as events turned out, bears favourable comparison with the amounts provided by Henry III of France and the States-General.

It is customary to describe Anjou's intervention in the Netherlands as a fiasco. While it seems likely that Anjou's own inadequacies would probably have ensured the same outcome even if he had been adequately financed [**doc. 14**], nevertheless his failure might not have been so abject if he had been given more support.

By the Treaty of Plessis-lès-Tours the States-General had agreed to pay Anjou 2,400,000 livres per year. Between May 1581 and October 1583 he realised only slightly more than half that amount from *all* his sources. In total, the States provided him with an amount which equalled less than two months' support. The excuse that the deputies gave was the great length of time it took for them to consult their constituencies before taxes could be levied.

In fact, Anjou was not popular. Holland and Zealand never got over their dislike of a Catholic prince as ruler. Brabant refused to pay him anything. There was no deception on the part of Orange; he simply could not control the individual provinces. As the States of Brabant lamented when Flanders fell to Parma in 1584, 'each province, preferring its own particular interest, has scarcely bothered about the fate of its neighbours and allies, thinking it enough to make fine promises on paper without following them up or giving them any effect' (**80**, p. 216).

Anjou himself thought he had been 'made a Matthias' by the Netherlanders, and in retaliation for his shabby treatment he planned to seize Antwerp and other principal towns in Flanders. However, his attempt to capture Antwerp with 3,500 men failed ignominiously. Even then Orange attempted to negotiate a new agreement between Anjou and the States, but Anjou had lost confidence in the Netherlanders and he left for good at the end of June 1583, leaving his troops to fight on as mercenaries.

Orange, despairing of ever controlling the States, moved to Holland. He once more persuaded the States-General to negotiate a treaty with Anjou in April 1584, which promised the duke more authority, but Anjou died before he could sign it. Thus, there was no effective central leadership in the United Provinces. At this critical juncture the quarrelsome States might have turned to Orange to create an effective government for the Republic, but the fifty-one-year-old prince was assassinated in Delft on 10 July 1584 by a royalist fanatic. Everyone knew that there was no one in the United Provinces who could replace Orange, and the States-General was forced once more to seek outside help.

# 6 The Birth of the Dutch Republic to the Twelve Years' Truce, 1584–1609

## Elizabeth I and the Armada: another turning point?

In 1581 Parma had calculated that he only had to occupy the Flemish coast and blockade the River Scheldt above Antwerp to undermine the economies of the important towns of Brabant and Flanders and force the rebel provinces to surrender. When the Walloon provinces allowed him to recall the Spanish troops in 1582, he began to put this plan into effect. After a string of victories in which town after town fell to his forces, Parma eventually forced Ghent to surrender on 17 September 1584, by which time he controlled almost the whole of Flanders. He then concentrated on blockading Brussels, which fell to him on 10 March 1585. He constructed a bridge across the Scheldt and although rebel fire-ships blew a hole in it on 5 April, he still managed to use the routeway to blockade Antwerp, which surrendered to him on 17 August without a shot being fired on the city.

Thus in three years Parma had doubled the area of the 'obedient' provinces. Many of the towns were captured through treachery, as ill-feeling towards the States-General increased when it became clear that it was not prepared to send relief forces to oppose Parma. Yet it was also clear that the prince had the ability to overcome the special military and strategic problems posed by the geography of the Netherlands. Philip II was justified in thinking that it was only a matter of time before the rebel provinces succumbed to the might of Parma's reconquest and he refused to allow the prince to offer any concessions on religion [**doc. 6**].

Fortunately for the beleaguered United Provinces, Elizabeth I felt compelled, at last, to intervene directly in the Netherlands to prevent a full Spanish conquest. There were a number of reasons for Elizabeth's decision. One was the fear that if Philip II fully controlled the Netherlands he would almost certainly invade England and depose the queen. As early as the 1530s, when Henry VIII broke with the Papacy, there had been calls on Spain to intervene in English affairs. At the Spanish court, 'interventionists' argued the need for an invasion to preserve the Catholic faith in England. Philip generally took the advice of those who argued for caution, on the grounds that there was no evidence that such an 'enterprise' had much support and that it risked Spain being involved in a lengthy and costly civil war in England (**2**).

However, Elizabeth knew that after Philip II's brief experience of England in 1558, the Spanish king felt more responsible for the preservation of the Catholic faith there, and that he had begun to consider the invasion plans more seriously. Elizabeth was aware that Philip had given his approval for the Ridolfi Plot* in 1571 and that he had contemplated a naval expedition against England in 1574. She also knew that Philip resented England's piratical interventions in the empire of the Indies and that he was incensed by the support she gave Dom António, the Portuguese claimant who had been exiled after Spain's occupation of Portugal in 1580–83. Yet it was England's meddling with the rebellion in the Netherlands which angered Philip the most. Affairs here came to a head in late 1584 when, partly because of the discovery of Spanish involvement in the Throckmorton plot to murder the queen, but mostly as a result of the deaths of Anjou and Orange, Elizabeth offered military aid to the United Provinces.

The States quarrelled amongst themselves about the conditions they ought to impose on Elizabeth, but on 9 August 1585 it was agreed that she could provide a Governor-General who would, on the advice of a new Council of State, direct the war and co-ordinate government. In return, Elizabeth promised to send a sizeable army to relieve Antwerp and, in addition, to pay the States 600,000 florins a year. As security, Elizabeth gained control of Flushing, Rammekens and Brill. These details were finalised in the Treaty of Nonsuch, which was signed on 20 August. Despite the loss of Antwerp, Elizabeth gradually built up the English presence in Holland to 8,000 men by December 1585. Before Christmas, the earl of Leicester was sent to Flushing to command the force and become Governor-General, and Francis Drake was dispatched to the Caribbean to plunder Spanish shipping in order to provide the necessary finance (**3**).

The fact that Elizabeth did not declare formal war against Spain needs further explanation. For a number of years there had been a running debate in the Queen's Privy Council about intervention in the Netherlands. In 1580 the Spanish occupation of Portugal and Drake's return from the circumnavigation voyage provided support for those advisers who wanted military aid to be sent to the Dutch rebels. These 'interventionists' argued that if England supported the attempts of the exiled Dom António to regain power in Portugal, Philip would have to divert more resources from Flanders and would thus give Elizabeth's troops more-opportunity to establish themselves securely in the Netherlands. Furthermore, they argued, Drake's success had demonstrated the vulnerability of the Empire in the Indies to piratical raids, and this lent weight to those who wanted England to adopt a more aggressive foreign policy based on commercial warfare.

While Elizabeth was prepared to threaten Philip with this possibility, she was realistic enough to know that economic warfare was double-edged and that England's position was equally vulnerable. The queen supported a compromise settlement in the Netherlands by which Philip II would retain sovereignty in the Netherlands in return for evacuating his troops, granting provincial self-government and conceding freedom of conscience. Elizabeth also thought that a moderate settlement would reduce the threat posed to international Protestantism by the Catholic League in France which, together with the Pope and the Habsburgs, had sought Spain's help in extirpating Protestantism from Europe and from England in particular. Thus Elizabeth wanted to prevent Spain from reconquering the Netherlands, but was afraid of the consequences of a full-scale war with Spain and sought a negotiated settlement.

Between 1578 and 1585, in order to avoid open war with Spain, Elizabeth tried to persuade France to take up arms in support of the Dutch rebels. However, England's relations with Anjou and Henry III caused a good deal of tension in the Privy Council and a number of questions were hotly debated: should Elizabeth allow Anjou to become Governor of the Netherlands? should she even co-operate with him? could the queen engineer a conflict between France and Spain which could then be exploited to defend the rebel cause? could Anjou be trusted? would Henry III really support Anjou? was it too dangerous for Elizabeth to propose marriage with Anjou merely to retain his support for an anti-Spanish policy in the Netherlands? Only in 1585, when Henry III refused to accept sovereignty in the Netherlands, did Elizabeth and her advisers finally put this 'French option' to one side.

By then, the Privy Council had agreed that English intervention in the Netherlands was unavoidable. Anjou had died, and with the assassination of William of Orange in October 1584, the Netherlands appeared to be on the brink of total political collapse.

Elizabeth offered the rebels limited military assistance in order to restore the political stalemate in the Netherlands. She hoped that Philip could still be brought to accept her moderate proposals for a settlement. Indeed, with the aim of coaxing Philip to the negotiating table, the queen maintained contacts with Spain in 1586 and 1587. Her policy seemed on the verge of success in the spring of 1588 when Philip agreed to a conference at Bourbourg in Flanders. However, neither the Dutch rebels nor the Spanish king were prepared to accept Elizabeth's proposals, and the conference failed to achieve a settlement.

Philip had viewed Elizabeth's military intervention in the Netherlands as an act of war, and it fuelled the arguments of those amongst his advisers who wanted to launch an 'enterprise' against England. Parma had warned Philip II that the reconquest of the rebel provinces could not continue whilst England supported them, but the duke did not have confidence in the invasion plans that Philip drew up. He thought them ill-thought-out and unrealistic. The king had to order him to deploy his troops in readiness for embarkation to England. In the end Parma's fears were justified. Not only were Philip's battle plans ill-conceived, but he had not thought out his strategy in the event of a victory. He gave no indication of his intentions regarding the English succession and he took no steps to help organise a Catholic rising in England prior to the invasion. His concerns appeared to be centred on the strategic demands of empire and not on recapturing England for the Catholic Church. The secret orders that Philip issued to Parma in the event of naval defeat indicate clearly that the king was more concerned to negotiate an English evacuation of the Netherlands than to obtain toleration for Catholics in England.

In May 1588 a 130-vessel Armada set sail from Lisbon and after numerous delays reached the Channel two months later. Its commander, Medina Sidonia, had orders to rendezvous with Parma's army and to mount a joint invasion of England. However, communications were poor and Parma's troops were not able to reach the embarkation point on time. At Gravelines, Medina Sidonia's ships suffered at the hands of the English gunners and afterwards a strong gale blew them out into the North Sea, from whence they tried to make their way back to Spain via the Fair Isle Channel between the Orkneys and the Shetlands. Many ships foundered on the coasts of Scotland and Ireland and their crews were often butchered by the locals. Only one-third of the 30,000 men who sailed from Lisbon returned home.

In terms of fighting power the defeat of the Armada was not the overwhelming blow to Philip II that many historians have claimed. Perhaps two-thirds of the Armada's fighting strength was saved and only four galleons (the largest type of ship) were lost. Within two years Philip was able to reconstruct his Indies fleets and could contemplate assembling another Armada. However, the 'enterprise of England' did mark a turning-point in the Dutch revolt. Philip II had failed to achieve his objectives, and although Leicester was recalled from the United Provinces and the rebels seemed vulnerable once more, Parma was not given the resources or the time to defeat them. Elizabeth's intervention in the Netherlands and the defeat of the Armada had forced Philip to consider alternative strategies for pressurising England and the Dutch. When Henry III died in 1589, Philip thought he could divert his forces from Flanders and, by defeating the Huguenots, take control of France. Such an eventuality would certainly have posed great problems for Elizabeth and the Dutch rebels. However, it proved to be a disastrous move for Spain.

## Leicester's brief Governorship

The Treaty of Nonsuch had allowed for the creation of a more effective central authority in the Netherlands, but Leicester found that the United Provinces were divided over how this might be achieved. The inland provinces wanted a more effective central authority to protect them from Parma, but Holland and Zealand feared that such an authority would threaten their provincial independence. However, the situation was more confused than this because there were differences of opinion within each of the provinces. Sensing that this disunity could prove fatal, Leicester attempted to impose his own plan which involved the creation of a stronger executive (with a special war treasury and new taxes independent of the States) and the implementation of a trade embargo against Spain and the obedient provinces. When Holland opposed the scheme in the summer of 1586, Leicester tried to rally the other provinces against her.

At this critical juncture Elizabeth summoned Leicester to England to advise her on whether or not to execute Mary Stuart. In his absence, two of his commanders betrayed Deventer to Parma (February 1587) and this act turned the provinces against the English plan. When he returned in March 1587, Leicester had new instructions: to persuade the States to negotiate with Parma.

However, in May, as the threat of an invasion of England grew, Elizabeth ordered Leicester's troops to return home and the States were free to disregard the new instructions.

Parma's reconquest of the north had been curtailed when it appeared that the United Provinces were on the verge of defeat. When Parma renewed his campaign in late 1588, he encountered stiffer opposition. The Dutch had strengthened their defence works along the river lines and the duke was unable to take Bergen-op-Zoom. Furthermore, Parma's troops were not paid regularly and on 30 August a spate of mutinies began, the first of over forty between 1589 and 1607. Faced with this crisis, Parma tried to persuade Philip II to open peace negotiations with the Dutch. He suggested offering the rebels the key concession of limited Calvinist worship in the towns of Holland and Zealand. Philip once again ruled out the idea of conceding toleration, but his advisers could see little alternative than 'a war without end'.

The Holy Roman Emperor offered to mediate between Philip II and the Dutch at another peace conference, but by 1591 the rebels sensed that the main thrust to reconquer the United Provinces had been thwarted and they hardened their attitude. They were helped by the fact that in July 1590 Philip II had intervened in the French Civil War and sent Parma and his army to Paris. In Parma's absence the Dutch leaders had ordered their new commander – Count Maurice of Nassau (William of Orange's second son) – to recover the towns in the north-east. In this he was most successful and Parma, who returned from France late in the summer of 1591 to try and stem the rebel victories, was unable to do anything. He was appalled at the loss of Spanish territory and openly disregarded Philip's orders to return to France. When he eventually and reluctantly obeyed his king, he was mortally wounded at the siege of Rouen and died in Arras in 1592.

Thus the English intervention, the Armada against England, and Spanish involvement in France had provided the Dutch with a much-needed respite from the reconquering troops of the duke of Parma. However, these events also created conditions which encouraged the rebel provinces to opt for self-governing independence. The Dutch experience of Matthias, Anjou and Leicester persuaded the rebel nobility and patricians that although they needed a figurehead to champion their cause, they did not require a ruler. The States-General and the Union of Utrecht had failed to protect towns against Parma, so it was fortunate that in Maurice of Nassau the rebel provinces had found an able commander. He was Stadholder of Holland and Zealand and from 1590–91 was also elected Stadholder of Gelderland, Overijssel and Utrecht. Maurice's cousin, William-Louis, was Stadholder of Friesland and, from 1594, of Groningen and Drenthe too. In this way the house of Orange-Nassau continued to provide leadership and some cohesion to the government of the United Provinces after Leicester's resignation in March 1588 had threatened to create chaos.

The States-General reduced the powers of the Council of State, and the States of the seven provinces of 1587–88 retained overall control. On 25 July 1590, they declared that the States-General was 'sovereign institution of the country, and has no overlord except the deputies of the provincial estates themselves'. The United Provinces had finally become the Dutch Republic.

## Political and constitutional arrangements

The new Dutch Republic was run by a close-knit oligarchy. The ruling class in the Republic as a whole comprised about 2,000 men who governed the provincial towns – the 'regent class' – and a minority of nobles. Each of the main towns, and especially those few with voting rights, was almost a city-state, ruled by a small group of magistrates. These officials were appointed from members of the city council which itself was composed of local patricians. The guilds usually had little influence on appointments to the city council, and the closed oligarchies of the towns made sure that they monopolised all the offices. The town councils seldom consulted with the guilds and other groups on matters of domestic policy. The guilds and local militia often sought to oppose the policies of the city oligarchs (as in Brussels in 1566 and 1572), but they rarely succeeded for long. Even so, a real 'public opinion' often existed and it would be wrong to assume that the voice of 'the people' was ignored by the regents. There were many printed newsletters (*corantos*), and a mass of controversial pamphlet literature, which served to keep the non-political nation critically informed of events and decisions.

However, after Leicester's resignation and the declaration of self-government, the States were entirely responsible to the towns they represented. Each of those towns that had gained the right to send delegates to the States also sent a deputation to each meeting of the provincial assembly with clear instructions as to how to vote. Only on the occasion of the assassination of William of Orange in

1584 was the inflexible method of referring back abandoned, and it was quickly reimposed. Representatives of the provinces in the States-General had to refer to their own States, and delegates in these States had to refer back to the oligarchs or nobles who had elected them. Thus, influential oligarchs in the voting towns could control the affairs not only of their own provinces, but also the States-General.

In this way the States-General became a small body often with not more than twelve deputies attending at any one time. These men were referred to as the 'Hogen-Mogen men', the 'High and Mighty'. In such circumstances, it proved easy for the deputies of Holland, the state that often paid up to two-thirds of the federal budget, to gain most influence and when, after 1593, the States-General met regularly in The Hague (the capital of Holland), this pre-eminence was almost taken for granted. Thus, *de facto* sovereignty in the Dutch Republic came to reside with the regents of the city councils of the eighteen 'voting towns' of Holland.

Gradually it was realised that this decentralised form of government was not conducive to the efficient administration of financial and military affairs in wartime. Thus the deputies of the States-General allowed Maurice of Nassau more and more executive responsibility as the field commander on the spot, and similarly allowed the experienced administrative 'colleges' of the States-General more freedom to deal with public finance and foreign policy – always with the proviso that any general decisions taken did not interfere with the domestic affairs of individual provinces. Little wonder that this system required politicians to be men of great common sense and tact, and that the leading spokesman – or 'advocate' – of the States of Holland came to have much influence. Between March 1586 and his death in May 1619, the post of advocate of Holland was filled by Johan van Oldenbarnevelt (**106**).

## The Spanish Netherlands

Parma's death left the seventy-five-year-old Count Mansfelt in charge in Brussels and Fuentes as commander-in-chief of the troops. Both men despised each other and both countermanded each other's orders. At the same time, the States of the obedient provinces baulked at using their resources to fight the French instead of the rebels, and in 1593 there were a number of riots when more money was demanded for the French war. There were also mutinies in the Spanish army. Thus in July 1593 the Brussels government was forced to negotiate a truce with the French Huguenot leader, Henry of Navarre. The truce of 1593–4 allowed Henry to consolidate his position in France first by prudently converting to Catholicism and then by capturing Paris. At the same time, the rebel provinces recaptured more towns, including Groningen (23 July 1594).

Philip II had tried to end the disunity in Brussels by appointing his nephew, Archduke Ernest, as governor, but the archduke died in February 1595, to be replaced by another of the kings's nephews – Archduke Albert – in 1596. Although Albert had some initial success, the Dutch soon negotiated a Triple Alliance with England and France at Greenwich which encouraged them to believe that their troops would capture more towns. In fact the Triple Alliance proved militarily disappointing. Archduke Albert had a good opportunity to exploit the weaknesses of the Alliance, but was thwarted by Philip's third bankruptcy, which was declared on 29 November 1596. Albert's troops, underpaid and underfed, began to lose heart, and in order to prevent wholesale desertions he ordered commanders to surrender if they came under heavy fire.

Late in 1597, Philip II reluctantly began peace negotiations with Henry of Navarre which resulted in the Peace of Vervins of May 1598. Since the Spanish king had already (in February) made a new settlement with his bankers, he was free once more to concentrate on England and the Dutch Republic. Philip did not live to see the results of this new campaign, for he died in September 1598. Nevertheless, he had made special provision for the Spanish Netherlands.

Philip had decreed that Spain and his other territories were to be governed by his son, who became Philip III. The king's daughter, Isabella, was to marry the Governor-General of Brussels – Archduke Albert – and the Netherlands were to be her dowry. The marriage took place in April 1599 and Albert and Isabella – together known as the 'Archdukes' – returned to Brussels in September.

Archduke Albert was the dominant partner: he had long experience of the workings of the Spanish court. However, the arrangements made the Archdukes dependent on Spain. They were dependent on Spanish troops and subsidies, and the 'collateral councils' in Brussels – the Councils of State and Finance and the Privy Council – had to accept decisions emanating from Philip III's court in Madrid or from the small group of Spanish advisers he appointed to act as a 'Spanish Ministry' in Brussels. The new king's desire to destroy the resistance of the rebel provinces and safeguard the obedient provinces overrode any thoughts of delegating more power to the Archdukes.

The position of the Archdukes was therefore not strong. One of Albert's earliest actions was to resume peace talks with the Dutch Republic. However, the rebels were not interested. They were alarmed that Federigo Spinola, a wealthy and influential Genoese sailor, had been sent to the Netherlands by Philip III to assemble a fleet of galleys to attack Dutch shipping and support a new invasion of England. Oldenbarnevelt ordered Maurice of Nassau to march into Flanders to destroy the Spanish bases. Neither the Spanish nor Dutch forces were particularly impressive in the ensuing fighting, but Maurice managed to capture Nieupoort. The Archdukes in retaliation ordered an attack on Ostend, but a siege required time and commitment, neither of which the Spaniards had. Mutinies in the army of Flanders and the death of Federigo Spinola nearly thwarted Albert's plans.

However, Federigo's brother, Ambrosio, now undertook to raise money and to lead an army in a siege of Ostend. After a long battle of attrition, Ostend fell in September 1604. In fact Maurice nearly stole Spinola's thunder when he captured the Sluis, but the siege of Ostend established Spinola's reputation as a commander and military entrepreneur. Certainly the Dutch had considered Ostend important enough for Oldenbarnevelt to travel to England in person in an attempt to persuade the new monarch – James I – to send troops to relieve the port. By the Treaty of Hampton Court, James promised Oldenbarnevelt that he and the new king of France – Henry of Navarre, now Henry IV – would support the Dutch with subsidies and allow the rebels to raise troops in England. However, this treaty was neutralised by the Treaty of London which the Spanish representatives concluded with James in August 1604, which effectively took England out of the firing line.

Under the terms of the Treaty of London, the English were still allowed to trade with the Dutch Republic and English traders in Spanish ports were guaranteed protection. The towns Elizabeth had controlled as a result of the Treaty of Nonsuch – the so-called cautionary towns – were now treated as neutral by Spain. English troops recruited by the Dutch under the terms of the Hampton Court treaty were permitted to continue serving in Maurice's army. Philip was prepared to make these concessions in order to prevent further English support for the Dutch rebels and to allow Spanish reinforcements to sail up the Channel.

At first, Philip III did not trust Spinola, but he valued Albert's tactical prowess even less, and in 1605 Spinola was allowed to take over all the archduke's military functions. As commander-in-chief, Spinola immediately led an army across the rivers Maas and Waal and attacked Overijssel. At this juncture the new commander went to Madrid and then Genoa to raise money for a campaign against Friesland. This gave Maurice the opportunity to consolidate his lines of defence, and so thoroughly did he accomplish this task that when Spinola renewed his campaign, in 1606, he could not make any headway. His money ran out and mutinies occurred in his army – one large contingent of 4,000 men actually set up an independent command at Diest. News of this setback dismayed Philip III, but he was powerless to help Spinola financially. The king was even forced to reduce the annual provision for the army of Flanders to 1.5 million ducats – barely sufficient for Spinola to finance a defensive war, let alone a major offensive to reconquer the northern provinces.

Luckily for Spinola, the Dutch too had found the latest campaigns burdensome. Expenditure by the northern provinces on the army had increased from 3.2 million florins in 1592 to 8.8 million in 1607. This, coupled with increases in levels of taxation and high interest payments on loans, forced the States-General to inquire of the Archdukes whether there were grounds for negotiating an armistice (though not, as yet, a full peace).

Oldenbarnevelt wanted the Archdukes to recognise the United Provinces as 'free lands, provinces and towns against which they claim nothing'. Yet there were those in the States-General, like Brederode, who thought the Catholic powers could not be trusted. This group wanted the war to continue, believing that there was an international conspiracy based on Madrid and Rome to destroy the privileges and ancient liberties of Protestant estates everywhere (**105**, Ch. 12). Nevertheless, an armistice was signed in March 1607. Oldenbarnevelt wanted the next round of negotiations to be conducted directly with Philip III, and although the king at first refused to treat with the rebels, his poor financial position forced him to send a personal representative to the talks.

There were a number of difficulties to be overcome. Philip was prepared to renounce Spain's sovereignty over the United Provinces but he was not willing to let the Dutch dictate terms about the rights and privileges of Catholics in the Republic, nor to accept

Dutch demands for trading rights in the Spanish colonies. He was all too well aware that since its inception in 1602 the Dutch East India Company had developed its illicit trade to such an extent that it was able to offer large dividends to its shareholders, which prompted some merchants to demand the formation of a parallel West India Company. Facing these difficult problems, Philip negotiated a six-month extension to the truce. In that time he hoped to exploit the growing differences between the inland provinces and Holland and Zealand to force the Dutch to reduce their demands. However, the militant Calvinists and merchants stood firm. This was partly because many ardent Calvinists had fled north to avoid Parma's reconquest, and they had strengthened the resolve of those who wanted the war to continue. In September 1608, Philip announced that he could not accede to the Dutch demands. The militants responded by declaring that further support of the truce was almost a treasonable offence. Renewal of war seemed inevitable.

At this juncture, Henry IV of France, afraid that he would be drawn into the fighting, suggested that if a full peace could not be arranged, it might be possible to agree a prolonged truce – perhaps for a period of twelve years. Since this more or less guaranteed the Dutch what they wanted, if only for a limited period, Oldenbarnevelt agreed. Maurice of Nassau, one of those who had favoured a continuation of the war, also agreed, knowing that his services as commander-in-chief could not be dispensed with.

However, there were still a number of merchants and Calvinists who opposed the move, and Oldenbarnevelt had to threaten to resign before the States-General finally agreed to proceed. In fact Philip III was himself not sure that a long truce was the solution, but his 'Spanish Ministry' in Brussels unanimously urged him to agree terms. It pointed out that an offensive war would cost about 300,000 ducats a month, a sum well beyond Philip's means, and that a defensive war would be a waste of time and threaten Spain's position in the obedient provinces. Philip finally agreed to the Dutch demands and a Twelve Years' Truce was ratified in Antwerp on 9 April 1609.

# 7 The Twelve Years' Truce, 1609–1621

It soon became clear to Spanish merchants that the terms of the Twelve Years' Truce would have disastrous consequences for Spain [**docs 19, 20**]. All obstacles to Dutch trade with Portugal and Spain had been removed; the blockade of the River Scheldt continued, to the detriment of Antwerp but to the advantage of Amsterdam; the Dutch came to dominate the north-south carrying trade, even penetrating regions in Spain (Valencia, Catalonia, Andalusia, Galicia and Portugal); the Dutch also increased their share of the Baltic trade to such an extent that by the 1620s their vessels accounted for two-thirds of all shipping entering the Danish Sound. Even more disturbing, from Spain's point of view, was the fact that the new Republic also expanded its operations in the East and West Indies, and their reputation as enemies of Spain also helped the Dutch to gain concessions from the Venetians and the Turks.

The main sectors of Spanish agriculture geared to export to Europe suffered and prices of certain crops, like wheat, were forced up, which encouraged local populations to ship in foreign, especially Baltic, grains. The Castilian cloth industry, already vulnerable to foreign competition at the turn of the century, now declined. As Sancho de Mancada complained in 1619: 'The damage to Spain arises from the new commerce of the foreigners, for in every prosperity [*i.e.* trade boom] in Spain, the foreigner intervenes and sucks it forth, depriving Spain of it and carrying it all to her enemies'. Such reverses fostered a popular Spanish mood highly unconducive to the renewal of the truce.

However, the truce was only beneficial to some groups and some provinces in the republic. The fears of the anti-truce faction were not removed. Taxation continued at high levels and there was actual commercial stagnation in southern areas of Holland and Zealand. Even more disturbing to the inland provinces was the revival of industrial activity in some areas of the obedient provinces, especially in Flanders and Brabant. Flemish woollens, linens, and other manufactures began to compete with Dutch products both in the Dutch local and re-export markets. Leiden lost its advantage over Hondschoote and Lille. Furthermore, English merchants managed to increase their share of the Dutch cloth market, forcing local Dutch manufacturers to concentrate more on the production of coarser cloth when it was least to their advantage to do so.

In many ways the Dutch were on better trading terms with Spain than they were with England, and during the period of the truce a number of disputes soured Anglo-Dutch relations. The English had Baltic, Levant and East India Companies of their own and competed with the Dutch in many areas of the world. English fishermen often complained that the Dutch took more than their share of the herring migration along the east coast of Scotland and in 1607 James I had banned the Dutch herring boats from English territorial waters. Nevertheless, such ill-feeling did not prevent Oldenbarnevelt negotiating the return of the cautionary towns in 1616 at the cost of a £100,000 down payment and three instalments of £50,000 at six-monthly intervals.

Thus there were grounds for opposition to Oldenbarnevelt's truce, and this sometimes expressed itself in urban disturbances as in 1616–17 in Delft, Haarlem, Utrecht, and Leiden. However, these disturbances also frightened the anti-Holland group of regents and nobles (led by Reynier Pauw and Prince Maurice), since they had no interest in fomenting social violence or encouraging sedition as such. What the anti-truce and anti-Holland faction in the States-General wanted was a broad national cause which was not socially divisive but which would allow the various social pressure to be channelled for specific political ends: the overthrow of Oldenbarnevelt and limitations on the power of the Holland regents and nobility. In time, it became clear that there were serious divisions of opinion within this 'opposition' faction, and there were those, like Maurice himself, who were jealous of the pre-eminence of Holland but were not against the Antwerp truce. Nevertheless, renewed religious dissension within the Republic provided the faction with an opportunity to combine their efforts against Oldenbarnevelt.

The majority of patricians in the towns had always been quick to condemn extreme religious groups and preachers because, in their view, religious conflict was a threat to their political position and to the authority of town councils. However, from the 1570s, many Calvinist clergy criticised the patricians for putting the affairs of the state before purity of doctrine and the establishment of the Kingdom of God on earth. For such Calvinists, the state was subordinate to the church. After 1609 this dispute merged with a very divisive theological debate concerning Calvin's view of predestination to create a political crisis in the Republic.

John Calvin had taught that God had predestined man's fate but that the majority of his own followers – the 'elect' – were destined to be saved (**89, 90**). As early as 1592, but especially in 1602 and 1608, Jacob Hermans or Arminius, a professor of theology at Leiden with liberal views, challenged this belief by arguing that Christ had died to save all souls, not just those of Calvin's so-called 'elect', and that in any case God allowed men a free choice whether to accept or reject His path to salvation. God, Arminius argued, was merciful. He would not predestine a man to hell. In fact Arminius believed that Calvin was correct in many of his other ideas and he remained a member of the Reformed Church until his death in 1609. However, on several occasions he was accused of heterodoxy and challenged to a public debate by the orthodox Calvinists led by Francis Gomarus. Initially the quarrel was settled by the civil authorities who wished to avoid an open schism in war-time, but the debate did not subside.

Supporters of Arminius continued after his death to answer the criticisms of their opponents in pamphlet form, but this only further inflamed passions and local synods demanded the dismissal of Arminians and the calling of a national synod to debate the issues. In Holland, where the debate was most bitter, the Arminians appealed to the provincial states for support, setting out their views in a written *Remonstrance*. Oldenbarnevelt was sympathetic, not because he agreed with Arminius over predestination, but because he favoured a state church established on broad foundations, one that did not alienate the Catholic majority or the Lutherans and Anabaptists [**doc. 7**]. Gomarus responded by publishing a *Counter-Remonstrance* to which most of the clergy subscribed.

The debate had many interested observers in England and it was to have a significant effect on developments in the English church and politics in the period before the Civil War. James I himself tried to intervene in support of the counter-remonstrants, despite Oldenbarnevelt's description of them as unruly Puritans* 'endeavouring in ecclesiastical matters . . . to usurp an extraordinary authority'. This made Oldenbarnevelt's position difficult. The orthodox Calvinists had watched with alarm the events taking place in nearby Jülich-Cleves and in Bohemia and north Italy, where Catholic powers seemed intent on destroying the independence of the

Protestant faith, and when Oldenbarnevelt endorsed the *Remonstrance*, the Calvinists thought he was helping the Catholic powers by diluting the purity of Calvinist faith and undermining the Prostestant movement generally. Calvinist clergy denounced Oldenbarnevelt as heretical and described the truce as a compact with the forces of evil. Even in Holland, Oldenbarnevelt faced opposition.

Although Amsterdam was the leading city of Holland, its city council had never trusted Oldenbarnevelt and had disliked the way he blocked their demands for the establishment of a West India Company which would have boosted their trading profits. The regents on the council now supported the counter-remonstrants and demanded the dismissal of Oldenbarnevelt and an end to the truce. For them, war was more profitable than peace. This was not the case with other provincial supporters of the *Counter-Remonstrance*, such as the Estates of Zealand, Friesland, Groningen and Gelderland. They were more interested in avoiding war and debating the theological issues in a national synod. Nevertheless, they disliked Oldenbarnevelt, and within months the advocate was outnumbered in the States-General by those who increasingly turned to Maurice of Nassau as the guardian of the counter-remonstrant cause. Oldenbarnevelt was obliged to defend himself and his province. Despite the opposition of Amsterdam he retained supremacy in Holland and in December 1616 managed to persuade the Estates to raise a force of militia – the *waardgelders*. Recruitment took place at Haarlem, Leiden, Gouda, Utrecht, Rotterdam and Schoonhoven.

This act offended the States-General and gave Maurice, the Stadholder, the opportunity to intervene directly in the affairs of Holland. In August 1618 he had Oldenbarnevelt arrested and then toured the towns of Holland at the head of his army removing those regents who had supported the advocate and the *Remonstrance*. In fact the 'new' men were of the same class as the 'old' since Maurice was not against the regent class in Holland as a class; he merely wanted to make himself, and the House of Orange, pre-eminent. Although he thought the regents of the coastal provinces were against the truce for their own interests and not those of the United Provinces as a whole, and although he was not convinced, as they were, that war was the best solution, he was not prepared to make the fundamental changes in the urban constitutions that the counter-remonstrants wanted.

Yet the Calvinists were not totally disappointed. Maurice

consented to their demands for the summoning of a national synod to draw up a new confession of faith. It met at Dordrecht (Dort) in 1618 and succeeded in cleansing the confession of all elements of Arminianism, and in effecting the dismissal of all Arminian clergy from their posts. The Calvinists also demanded the execution of Oldenbarnevelt, but Maurice desired only his submission, not his death. However, the advocate was accused of treason and, when he refused to confess, he was sentenced to death and beheaded (May 1619).

## The renewal of war

Spain could not ignore the economic reverses she suffered as a result of the truce. Nor could she ignore the many threats to her land-line of communications between the Ligurian coast and the Netherlands – known as the 'Spanish Road'. This routeway allowed Spanish troops to march northwards from Genoa into Lombardy and then across Savoy into Franche-Comte and Lorraine (which brought them dangerously close to the French stationed at Metz, Toul and Verdun). From Lorraine the Spanish troops could easily march into Luxembourg and then to Brussels or, via Jülich-Cleves and Münster, to Overijssel and Gelderland. Clearly this route was very vulnerable at certain points and a number of local crises between 1609 and 1621 involved Spain in military conflicts, some of which, like the Jülich-Cleves dispute, nearly initiated a European war.

The duchies of Jülich, Cleves, Mark, Berg and Ravensberg stretched along the river Rhine, and although ruled by one family were a mixture of religious persuasions. Jülich and Berg had remained Catholic; Mark and Ravensberg had converted to Lutheranism; while Cleves had become Calvinist. In 1609 the duke of Jülich-Cleves died without a male heir. Rudolf II, the Holy Roman Emperor, ordered his nephew, Leopold, to take possession of the duchies pending a full legal inquiry. However, the descendants of the late duke's sisters – John Sigismund, Elector of Brandenburg, and Wolfgang William, son of the Count Palatine of Neuburg – both claimed the duchies and agreed on a joint occupancy (the Treaty of Dortmund, 1609). The French and Dutch were drawn in to support the Protestant claimants and Maurice led a force to capture Jülich. With France ready to intervene, an international conflict seemed inevitable, but Henry IV was assassinated before he could launch a full-scale campaign and

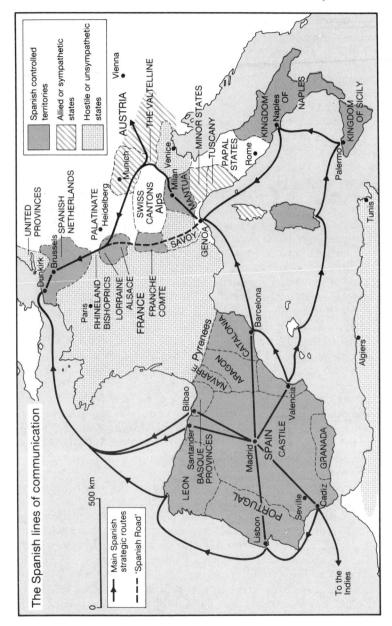

The Spanish lines of communication

Spanish controlled territories

Allied or sympathetic states

Hostile or unsympathetic states

Main Spanish strategic routes

'Spanish Road'

500 km

Vienna

THE VALTELLINE

AUSTRIA

KINGDOM OF NAPLES

NAPLES

KINGDOM OF SICILY

Palermo

Munich

Venice

MINOR STATES

TUSCANY

Rome

PAPAL STATES

Milan

MANTUA

SWISS CANTONS Alps

UNITED PROVINCES

SPANISH NETHERLANDS

PALATINATE

Heidelberg

Brussels

Dunkirk

SAVOY

GENOA

Tunis

RHINELAND BISHOPRICS

Paris

LORRAINE ALSACE

FRANCHE COMTE

FRANCE

Pyrenees

CATALONIA

Barcelona

Algiers

NAVARRE

ARAGON

Bilbao

Santander

BASQUE PROVINCES

LEON

Madrid

SPAIN

CASTILE

Valencia

GRANADA

PORTUGAL

Seville

Cadiz

Lisbon

To the Indies

73

the death of Rudolf II in 1612 led to a search for a compromise. In fact both the joint rulers changed their faiths in the hope of forwarding their claims, but none of the major powers was prepared for an all-out war and the two princes were persuaded to compromise by the Treaty of Xanten (November 1614). Yet the dispute clearly revealed to the Spanish and Dutch that religious divisions were hardening in Europe and that they were attracting foreign military and financial support.

The duke of Savoy-Piedmont was also a thorn in Spain's side in these years and could never be trusted. Spain failed to defeat the duke in 1614–15 and in 1616–17 when he tried to block the Spanish Road. In fact Spain had begun to bypass Savoy by using the route through the Adda valley, known as the Valtelline, which led from the frontier of the duchy of Milan through the Alps towards the Tyrol. However, this involved Spain in the political and religious conflicts of that area which once again often involved other outside powers, France in particular.

Spain was also anxious about the fortunes of the Austrian branch of the Habsburg family during the years of the truce which had seen an alarming turn of events in central Europe (**66**). Since the 1580s, Catholic rulers in Germany had been attempting to reconquer territory that had been lost to Protestantism largely as a result of the 1555 religious Peace of Augsburg, and the Catholic Reformation, boosted by the decrees of the Council of Trent\*, gave support to this new militancy. However, the Emperor Rudolf II (1576–1612) had allowed Habsburg power to wane and this had prompted the more militant members of the family, with support from Spain, to take matters into their own hands. Matthias (emperor 1612–19) began to improve Habsburg fortunes, but it was the rule of Ferdinand II (1619–37), a staunch Catholic, that really saw the Habsburgs in the ascendant in Europe as defenders of the Catholic faith.

Protestants in Europe had always feared the consequences of a rejuvenated Catholic reform movement and Calvinists were particularly vigilant in the watching brief they gave themselves as defenders of Protestantism. It was essentially Calvinists who had established a German Protestant (or Evangelical) Union in 1608 under the leadership of the Elector Palatine, Frederick V. This had been a great threat to the Habsburgs, since the Elector's territories, though in two parts (the Upper Palatinate between the River Danube and Bohemia, and the Lower Palatinate between the Rivers Mosel, Saar and Rhine) were near the centre of the Habsburg heartlands. The Catholics retaliated by forming a Catholic League in 1609 led by Maximilian of Bavaria. When it became clear that the Catholic League did not want the emperor to get involved, Spain began to support it herself for fear that Habsburg influence in Germany at this critical time would be fatally reduced.

This Spanish anxiety about the consequences of diminishing Austrian Habsburg authority was not allayed by further reverses, this time in eastern Europe, in Hungary (1604–6) and especially in Bohemia where there were rebellions against Emperor Rudolf II in 1609 and 1611. In May 1618 Bohemian nobles defied the emperor's authority again, claiming that concessions they had gained in 1609 and 1611 were being ignored. The Bohemians approached the Dutch rebels and the Protestant Union for help. The Dutch could only send money, but the Elector Palatine agreed to become king of Bohemia when the rebels 'deposed' Archduke Ferdinand (the king-designate and, from August 1619, Holy Roman Emperor). This act made the revolt a very serious challenge to Habsburg power in central Europe. Bohemia held the crucial seventh vote in the imperial election and if Frederick V, a Calvinist, became king, the Habsburgs would not only lose Bohemia but also control of the imperial title. The Catholic reform movement would suffer a major setback.

Spain could not ignore this threat and Philip III dispatched 750,000 florins to Vienna for the recruitment of troops. The papacy provided further subsidies for the emperor. Spain also sent about 10,000 troops from Italy and the Netherlands, and the latter, under Spinola, overran Frederick V's territory in the Lower Palatinate. The opponents of the Habsburgs could not match this show of strength and the Dutch were distracted by their internal political and religious crises. The Protestant German states remained neutral. Thus the emperor easily defeated the rebels at the Battle of the White Mountain near Prague in November 1620 and the Spanish troops retained control of Frederick's Rhine territories, forcing the luckless elector to flee into exile. This turn of events encouraged Philip III to believe that war with the Dutch rebels might result in a similar victory for Spinola.

Protestants throughout Europe, but especially in the Dutch Republic, viewed these moves with great alarm. Dutch and Palatine diplomats sought to create a great anti-Habsburg coalition of powers to defend themselves from what they saw as a joint Austro-Spanish attempt to establish a vast Habsburg-Catholic empire. Thus, when talks began between Spain and the Dutch Republic for renewing the truce, they took place within a European context that witnessed the merging of local struggles into a general European conflict – the beginnings, in fact, of the Thirty Years' War (**66**).

Spain had been preparing herself for the expiry of the truce almost as soon as it had been signed in 1609, and Spanish diplomats in foreign capitals attempted to create a durable chain of alliances: Gondomar in London, Bedmar (later known as Cardinal de la Cueva) in Venice, Cardenas in Paris, Osuna in Naples, Fuentes, Villafranca and Feria in Milan, and Baltasar de Zúñiga and Oñate in Vienna. Though they had been instructed by the duke of Lerma to seek diplomatic rather than military solutions to Spain's problems in Europe, most of these men came to blame the truce with the Dutch for Spain's reverses. They sought every opportunity to strengthen Habsburg influence in Europe and to safeguard the 'Spanish Road'. When Lerma fell from power in 1618 his 'peace policy' went with him.

For some time the Spanish nobility had disliked the way Lerma had monopolised the king's attention as *valido* or chief minister, especially since Philip III and Lerma spent much time away from the capital and the centre of government. These absences had led to a restoration of conciliar government where councils and special committees (*juntas*) dealt with most business. However, as Spain suffered reverses abroad demand grew for a change of foreign policy and for the king to take more personal control at home. The opposition to Lerma had formed alliances around Lerma's own son, the duke of Uceda, and, in the important council of state, deferred to the views of the count of Olivares and Zúñiga, both of whom opposed Lerma. When Lerma fell, the king retained most of his executive and patronage powers for himself, and Uceda never achieved the status of *valido*. Olivares and Zúñiga were able to persuade the king to maintain a hard-line foreign policy in northern Europe (**125**).

In April 1619 Zúñiga wrote to Philip III advising him that the confrontation in the Netherlands could not be isolated from the conflict unfolding in central Europe, and that, given the intricacies of the European situation and the known difficulties of campaigning in the Netherlands, it was time to acknowledge the fact that, as far as the United Provinces were concerned, the restoration of Spanish rule and the Catholic faith by force of arms was not possible [**doc. 21**]. Yet paradoxically, he was fervently against renewing the truce on its existing terms: 'if the republic of these rebels goes on as it is, we shall succeed in losing first the two Indies, then the rest of Flanders, then the states of Italy and finally Spain itself'. If the truce could not be improved, he argued, then war, even a war without end, was preferable to the humiliation, loss of prestige, and the passivity which had resulted from the 1609 agreement.

Philip III sought the views of a large number of people, but his advice to Archduke Albert in February 1621 was principally that of Zúñiga. Albert had written to the king in December 1620 trying to persuade Philip not to seek a military solution in the Netherlands: 'I see Your Majesty entangled in Bohemia, in the Palatinate and, through the Valtelline affair, in Italy, and were you to take on your shoulders a war in these provinces with Holland this summer you would find it a heavy piece of work'. Philip's reply ordered Albert not to extend the existing truce without securing Dutch withdrawal from the Indies and the lifting of the blockade of the Scheldt, conditions which were unacceptable to the Dutch. Philip, though still anxious to press for Spanish sovereignty and toleration for Catholics in the Netherlands, was more concerned with the economic consequences of the truce which, he told Albert, might 'prove the total ruin of these realms' if it was extended.

Albert had been convinced that Maurice was prepared, with French mediation, to reduce the rebel provinces once more to obedience to Spain in return for renewing the truce of 1609. Albert knew that the five inland provinces of Overijssel, Utrecht, Friesland, Groningen, and Gelderland, were not against the truce and were against war. The Arminians also expressed their support for a settlement. Against the king's orders Albert sent his chancellor – Pecquius – to put a proposal formally to the States-General (**54**). However, the States-General rejected Albert's proposal and the 9 April deadline for the termination of the truce passed without a settlement being achieved.

It is customary to describe how matters were brought to a head in March 1621 when Frederick V, the exiled Elector Palatine, arrived in the Hague. It is true that Maurice presented the Elector and his entourage as victims of a Catholic and Habsburg conspiracy which threatened to engulf all Europe and he argued that the Habsburgs had to be combatted on a wide front. However, it was not Maurice's wish to provoke a renewal of the war with Spain. He wanted other powers to intervene to distract Spain's attention from the Netherlands and thereby diminish the military threat. Even after the death of Philip III on 30 March, Maurice continued to negotiate in secret with Spanish representatives in Brussels, and led them to believe that he would make concessions over the blockade of the Scheldt if the truce could be renewed. Albert communicated his impressions to Madrid, stressing once again how difficult it would be to fight an offensive war against Maurice. This made Zúñiga even more pessimistic about Spain's ability to subdue the rebel provinces by force of arms, but he remained convinced that the truce could not be renewed as it stood. Thus the truce was not extended or altered. Archduke Albert died in July 1621, and Philip IV brought the southern Netherlands more directly under Spanish control by sending Bedmar to be Isabella's chief adviser, and mouthpiece for the king's decisions. On 30 July the Spanish Council of State encouraged the king to re-open hostilities, and the king followed its advice and duly communicated his decision to Isabella via Bedmer.

# 8 War with Spain, 1621–1648

In cost and scale the new round of fighting between the Dutch Republic and Spain was equal to the encounters of the first round in the sixteenth century, yet there were significant differences. After 1627 both sides came to the conclusion that an outright victory by way of vigorous land campaigning and territorial conquest was out of the question. The struggle on land was reduced to *guerra defensiva*\* – a struggle to maintain defensive lines around the southern approaches to the rivers Maas and Waal. Quick victories, as Spinola lamented, were precluded by the vast nature of siege operations: 'In order to capture a rebel town, an entire summer and army may be consumed without any certain success' (**93**, p. 86). The struggle at sea proved costly for the Dutch as well as the Spanish, especially in the East and West Indies, and it was the failure of the West India Company which encouraged the Amsterdam merchants to sue for peace in the 1640s.

Furthermore, from the early 1620s, Philip IV and his chief minister, Olivares, attempted to force the Dutch economy into bankruptcy by employing a policy of economic blockade and the imposition of trade embargoes using the armada of Flanders in operations against Dutch merchant shipping and the North Sea fisheries (**53, 54, 125**). The Spanish also hoped to re-open the navigation of the river Scheldt and revive the flagging fortunes of Antwerp as a counter to Amsterdam. These Spanish economic policies were part of a wider plan to establish Habsburg dominance in western and northern Europe, linking the naval prowess of Spain with the new-found military power of the Austrian Habsburgs under Albrecht Wallenstein. They were to have disappointing results, and the blockade proved just as damaging to the Spanish economy as it did to that of the Dutch. As if to reflect the inconclusive nature of the encounters, truce soundings ran in parallel with the fighting and both sides tried to exploit their latest advance to strengthen their bargaining position in the regular rounds of peace negotiations.

After 1621 there were different strategic and financial constraints for the Dutch and Spanish to contend with. Both combatants had insufficient resources for the type of campaign that would ensure total victory. In the Republic, during the 1620s alone taxes increased by almost 50 per cent, a state of affairs which aroused the indignation of the populace and led to a number of disturbances in some towns. The States of Holland, which provided two-thirds of the war budget, preferred to fight a defensive war against Spain and were most reluctant to finance offensive campaigns. It is also not clear that the Republic, already over-dependent on English and Scottish seamen and soldiers, had sufficient manpower to undertake and sustain a vigorous land war as well as a naval and commercial one.

The Spanish government proved very adept, throughout the first half of the seventeenth century, at raising loans, armies and armadas, but after 1621 it was faced with fighting on a number of fronts at the same time as the war against the Dutch merged with other conflicts in central and northern Europe to create the Thirty Years' War (**66**). Apart from a number of early sorties by Spinola, Spain was unable to commit the bulk of her forces to the Dutch theatre of the European war for long. For instance, in 1629 the War of the Mantuan Succession in northern Italy forced Spain to divert resources away from the Dutch struggle. In 1630 the king of Sweden, Gustavus Adolphus, invaded central Europe and, until his death at the Battle of Lutzen in 1632, threatened to defeat the Austrian Habsburgs and completely undermine Spain's position in western Europe. Spain felt compelled to help the emperor as much as she could, and even after 1632 the Swedes remained a dangerous force in Europe, often drawing Spanish troops away from the Netherlands. In 1635, France entered the Thirty Years' War against the Habsburgs, but against Spain in particular. This necessitated a massive redeployment of Spanish troops and once again prevented Spain from concentrating her forces against the Dutch. The Dutch were quick to exploit the European situation for their own ends and were diplomatically active in all the major European capitals in an attempt to gain military aid from Denmark, England, Sweden and France. Thus, Spain was severely constrained in her encounters with the Dutch in this second round of fighting (**125**).

Initially, both Maurice and Spinola had ambitious plans. Maurice wanted to reconquer the Spanish Netherlands and perhaps to restore Frederick V to the Palatinate. Spinola wanted to exploit his successful intervention in the Rhineland by invading the northern provinces, a plan which caused consternation in

Madrid where the king's advisers foresaw financial ruin if the fighting did not produce quick results. Spinola acted first in 1622 by attacking Bergen-op-Zoom. The attack was repulsed, but in 1624 the Spaniards laid siege to the strategically and symbolically important city of Breda. Maurice died just as the siege began and his half-brother and successor, Frederick Henry, was unable to prevent Breda falling to Spinola in June 1625.

The government in Madrid was delighted, but Frederick Henry was a skilful commander and he prevented the Spaniards from marching northwards to exploit their victory. Relations between Spain and England deteriorated in 1624 and this denied the Spanish supply ships and troop transports the shelter they needed for a further attack on the north. Also in 1624, the Swiss Protestants of the Valtelline gained control of this important valley on Spain's vital new land route to the Netherlands and this forced an interruption in Spinola's offensive.

Furthermore, by the end of 1625 Dutch diplomats had succeeded in creating an anti-Habsburg coalition of powers – the Hague Coalition – involving England and Denmark. The Dutch agreed to provide 50,000 florins a month to maintain 30,000 infantry and 8,000 cavalry in north Germany with the object of liberating the Rhineland and curbing the recent military successes of the Habsburgs in central Europe. Denmark intervened directly and the Danish king, Christian IV, led an army into northern Europe ostensibly to fight the Habsburgs on behalf of the Coalition, but really to secure the king's own interests in northern Europe and to counter any move by Sweden, Denmark's arch-rival in the Baltic, to gain territory along Germany's northern coast. The Danish intervention was a fiasco and the Danes were routed by the combined forces of the emperor and the Catholic League led respectively by Wallenstein and Tilly. The Treaty of Lubeck of June 1629 forced Denmark to withdraw from the Hague Coalition and left Wallenstein in control of northern Germany. It was only the intervention of the Swedish king, Gustavus Adolphus, in 1630, which saved the life-line of the Dutch economy, the trade between Amsterdam and Danzig (**66**).

England's role in the anti-Habsburg coalition was not as effective as the Dutch might have expected. After the Treaty of London (1604), James I allowed a significant proportion of Elizabeth's forces to be transferred to the service of the States-General, and in 1616 these were supplemented by the garrisons of the old cautionary towns. By 1621 there were two Scottish and four

English regiments in the service of the States (a force of 13,000 men, a third of the Dutch standing army). However, James also allowed Spain to recruit among English Catholics and during the 1620s and 1630s there were on average 4,000 British troops in the army of Flanders. This revealed that neither James I nor Charles I was committed to the defence of the Dutch rebels or in favour of leading a European Protestant alliance. Both monarchs were aware that many of their subjects believed in the existence of a papal-led Catholic plot for the extirpation of heresy, and that the Bohemian revolution of 1618 and the subsequent Palatine war demanded a strengthening of the Anglo-Dutch alliance and support for the Hague Coalition. However, both James and Charles regarded a religious war as a potential disaster which had to be avoided, and they were more interested in securing a general ecumenical settlement of the European confessional confrontation, and in preserving England's role as mediator in European affairs (1).

The failure of the Spanish marriage alliance* only temporarily led to a hardening of attitudes against Spain. James I continued to respect Spanish honour and have contempt for French unreliability, and although Charles I (who succeeded his father in 1625) reacted to his humiliating experience in Madrid in 1623 by supporting plans for a war against Spain, his basic attraction towards a Habsburg alliance soon reasserted itself. In 1624, the duke of Buckingham* attempted to cement a marriage alliance with France in the expectation that this would secure French military assistance against Spain in the Netherlands and the Palatinate. Not waiting to see how the French reacted to his ideas, Buckingham promised King Christian IV of Denmark and the Dutch that England, with French support, would join the Hague Coalition against Spain.

However, although Louis XIII was anxious to enter an anti-Habsburg coalition, he was constrained by staunch Catholics at his court (the *dévots*), who argued that France could not join the coalition because it was motivated by the defence of the Protestant cause. The French king was also annoyed that Buckingham had been so presumptuous, and in February 1626 he signed a peace with Spain (the Treaty of Monzón). Buckingham was furious and persuaded Charles to send a naval expedition to La Rochelle to support a Huguenot rebellion against Louis XIII and his minister Richelieu. The expedition was badly mismanaged and Buckingham was forced to use money initially raised to support the Dutch rebels. Fortunately for England, Buckingham was assassinated in August 1628 and a treaty was concluded with Richelieu at Suza in May 1629. However, Charles also extricated himself from the Hague Coalition by concluding a treaty with Spain in Madrid in November 1630, by which Philip IV provided written assurance that in the event of a general settlement of the European conflict, Frederick V, Charles's brother-in-law, would be restored to the Palatinate.

When Gustavus Adolphus invaded Germany in 1630, many of Charles's advisers argued that England should support the Swedes. Charles, however, felt this would undermine the agreement he had recently made with Spain. Even when Philip IV wanted Charles to declare war against the Dutch as the price of a Palatine restoration, the English king continued to refrain from entering an anti-Habsburg coalition. Thus the Dutch were disappointed by the attitude of the first two Stuart monarchs and it was fortunate for them that Spain could not mount a decisive campaign against the rebels.

However, if Spain was not able to concentrate all her military might against the Dutch after the opening of the Thirty Years' War, she certainly attempted to challenge the Dutch economic and commercial predominance established during the Twelve Years' Truce. An important part of this process involved a naval blockade of the Republic and the exclusion of Dutch ships from Spanish ports. One way the Dutch attempted to get round this exclusion was to send goods in neutral ships. To counteract this ploy the Spaniards set up a Northern Board of Admiralty (*almirantazgo*) in 1624 to inquire into the origins of cargoes and to issue licences. This Board was supported by an armada of thirty galleons which patrolled the English Channel and North Sea, and harassed Dutch shipping. Privateers operating from Dunkirk found they could easily undermine the work of the Dutch herring fleets and the Spaniards encouraged them. The Admiralty Board and the privateers were so successful that between 1629 and 1638 about 1,000 Dutch ships were sunk and almost 2,000 were captured. Freight charges and marine insurance premiums increased rapidly, to the detriment of Dutch commerce. English and French merchants were quick to exploit these setbacks and Dutch textiles in particular experienced a damaging slump.

However, the Spanish economy was equally vulnerable to exclusion policies and naval blockades, and the Dutch countered the *almirantazgo* policy with a blockade of Dunkirk – the pirates' base – and, in 1639, soundly defeated a Spanish fleet in the Battle of the Downs to secure continuation of Dutch freedom of operation in Flemish waters. Yet Spain's *almirantazgo* policy proved very effective, and there is little doubt that had she been able to maintain her grip on Dutch trading operations, Spain would have forced the Dutch to sue for peace on Spain's terms. However, Spain depended quite heavily on Dutch shipping for imports and exports, and the Spanish Netherlands had to be allowed to continue to trade with the north to avoid undermining Flemish industry. Gradually Spain was forced to allow Dutch ships to enter southern Spanish ports to provide grain, but it was not until 1647 that the economic blockade was officially lifted.

The Dutch were always adept at defending themselves. Frederick Henry soon proved himself to be a force to be reckoned with. In 1626 he captured Oldenzaal and by 1629 he had captured the Rhineland fortress of Wesel, and 's Hertogenbosch in Brabant. As a consequence of these events, the southern Netherlands once more considered uniting with the northern provinces, but the Catholics were alarmed by the way the Calvinists dealt with their co-religionists in 's Hertogenbosch and this rare opportunity to unite the Netherlands was allowed to pass.

A leading Flemish nobleman – van der Bergh – defected to the north in 1632, hoping thereby to effect a closer union of the north and south, but his appeal to his countrymen to rise in revolt had little effect. However, the Spaniards recognised that his defection needed to be taken seriously and they called a States-General of the southern provinces. The States wanted peace negotiations to be opened with the north. Yet the negotiations which opened in 1634 soon foundered over the rights of Catholics in the republican provinces and a demand by the Dutch that Philip IV assist them in America (**54**).

This last demand by the Dutch reflected the turn of events in the conflict overseas. In 1621 a group of Amsterdam merchants, many of whom had fled there from the south in the sixteenth century, had succeeded in establishing a West India Company with the principal aim of trading in the West Indies. The States-General had always opposed such a development, but in wartime it recognised that the company's military activities were strategically very important and agreed to provide it with naval support. The States were immediately rewarded for their efforts when, in 1624, Piet Heyn seized Bahia, the capital of Brazil. Yet the Spanish reacted quickly to this setback and within ten months a Spanish army had compelled the Dutch to surrender their prize.

This turn of events nearly bankrupted the West India Company, but privateers like Heyn continued to plunder the Caribbean and provide company directors with the resources to pay their shareholders high dividends. For instance, in 1628 Heyn captured the entire Spanish silver fleet in Matanzas Bay (Cuba), and this allowed the directors to declare a dividend of 50 per cent. The company used some of its profits to raise and equip a strong expeditionary force which was used to attack Recife in Pernambuco with the aim of gaining control of the rich sugar plantations in its vicinity. Yet the directors had underestimated the difficulties involved in their greed to maximise profits, and the predominantly Portuguese settlers on the plantations defended themselves well. The ensuing fighting lasted six years and drained the company of its profits. This encouraged the States-General of the northern provinces to enter the abortive peace negotiations of 1634.

The Dutch were more successful in the East Indies and managed to capture a good slice of Spanish trade in the region. From new bases in Sri Lanka and Malacca, Dutch traders increased their links with Chinese and Indian merchants. However, Spain retained control of Manila and Macao, and never allowed the Dutch to undermine her trade completely.

The Spanish government decided to send another large army to the Netherlands in an effort to bolster the defence of the obedient provinces and curb the ambitions of Frederick Henry. The Cardinal-Infante Ferdinand, victor over the Swedes at the Battle of Nordlingen in central Europe, arrived in Brussels in 1635 to lead the army, a move which caused consternation in the Republic. Frederick Henry proposed an alliance with France in the hope that Ferdinand could be distracted from invading the north. However, the Cardinal-Infante was dismayed by the poor state of the Spanish troops in the Netherlands and he thought a quick victory against the Republic was not possible. Even more alarming for him, later in the same year France decided that her policy of war by diplomacy in western Europe had failed to curb Habsburg power and she declared war against Spain. The Dutch were saved once again (**124**).

Frederick Henry was skilled in the arts of siege warfare but not in commanding the Dutch fleet. Although he was made Admiral-General, the real commander of the fleets was Maerten Tromp, who had much more experience of naval tactics and strategy. He was given authority to reform the navy and in 1639 the States-General was delighted to hear that his forces had destroyed a

Spanish relief fleet in the neutral waters of the Downs in the Channel (October 24). Some members of the States-General now began to consider Spain a spent force in Europe and demanded a more vigorous naval campaign in the New World. This view was strengthened by the defeat of a flotilla of Spanish and Portuguese ships near Pernambuco in January 1640. However, those who supported a continuation of the war on land were also given a boost by a number of reverses in Spain's fortunes.

The government in Madrid, alarmed at the increasing demands made upon Castilian resources as a result of Spain's involvement in the European war, had since 1627 attempted to implement Olivares's plan for a Union of Arms (**31, 33**). This plan involved persuading the other four kingdoms of the Spanish monarchy to contribute their fair share of the costs of the war. It also came to embrace Spain's satellites such as Milan, Naples, and Sicily. Bullion imports from the New World had been important in enabling the government to secure loans, but they never represented more than a fraction of the funds raised by the treasury in other ways. However, the policy failed to get much response from the other kingdoms. Catalonia, in particular, resented the Castilianisation of the monarchy and, in 1640, revolted against the Castilian troops that Madrid had sent to defend the Catalans from the French. In January 1641 a joint French-Catalan army defeated the Castilians outside Barcelona, an event which encouraged the Dutch to continue fighting. But for the impressive support of Naples and Sicily, Spain's struggle for survival would have ended in failure (**125**).

Spain also faced problems in Portugal. Late in 1640 the duke of Braganza led a revolt to support his claim to the throne and prevent Castile's centralising policies from undermining the rights and privileges of the Portuguese nobility. In December, Braganza declared himself King John IV of Portugal. In January 1641, his brother-in-law, Medina Sidonia, attempted to take control of Andalusia and assert its independence. Although he was unsuccessful, Sidonia's action was a further indication to the Dutch that the Spanish monarchy was threatened with disintegration from within. The Spaniards were thrown into more confusion when the Cardinal-Infante died in November 1641. Although Philip IV quickly replaced him with Don Francisco de Melo, it was becoming clear to Madrid that Spain's relations with the Dutch needed a fundamental reappraisal. The chief victim of this process was Olivares. Philip IV bowed to aristocratic pressure for his *valido's* dismissal in 1643, a move which forced the king to rule more in his own right (**125**).

## The drive for peace, 1641–48

Most of Philip IV's ministers agreed that every effort should be made to conclude either a full peace or a truce with the Dutch, although they were aware that recent Spanish reverses would make the task very difficult to accomplish. Even the king's promise to recognise Dutch Brazil, refusal of which had been a major stumbling block in earlier negotiations, did not succeed in inducing the States-General to enter new talks. Before his dismissal, Olivares advised Philip of the need for caution in making concessions in case Spain's rush to conclude a settlement created more problems than it solved (**33**).

Prince Frederick Henry remained inclined to continue the war in alliance with the French, though the Spanish diplomats sensed his commitment was not strong and that, if pressed, he might be persuaded to negotiate a peace. The Dutch provinces were not united in their support of the war and Philip IV felt that to convince the prince of the need for peace would also be sufficient to persuade the States-General to begin negotiations. Thus in secret negotiations in April 1642, Melo promised the prince that in return for a peace, Philip IV would even concede to the Dutch freedom of commerce with the Spanish empire, both in Europe and the Indies (**54**, p. 349). The prince interpreted this offer as a clear sign that Spain was getting desperate and he responded coolly, hoping the Spanish negotiators would make more concessions. However, the European war had already reached the point where the combatants were more anxious to search for an honourable peace than to launch more expensive campaigns, and the Dutch-Spanish negotiations now became part of the general drift towards peace in Europe.

As early as 1638 (with the Treaty of Hamburg) the major European powers had sought to establish a series of peace conferences. By December 1641, France, Sweden, Spain, and the new emperor (Ferdinand III) had agreed to begin peace talks in two separate gatherings, at Münster and Osnabrück. Frederick Henry persuaded the Dutch States to send plenipotentiaries to the talks in Münster. It appeared that Europe was on the verge of concluding a general peace settlement. Yet rivalry over procedure between the great powers, and also between the Dutch provinces and towns, delayed the start of the peace conferences until July 1643. As late as May 1643 the provinces had not finalised their recommendations to the States-General. Relations between Holland and Frederick Henry became strained and once again Philip IV secretly made proposals to the prince.

This time Philip promised Frederick that the prince and his heirs would be recognised as rulers of a northern Netherlands state based on Holland but excluding Zealand (which was to be transferred to the Spanish Netherlands to relieve Antwerp) and 's Hertogenbosch, the Maas towns and Nijmegen. Dutch Brazil was to be returned to Spain and Spanish Catholics were to have freedom of worship. The prince himself was to hold his territories as a form of enfeoffment either from the Spanish monarchy or the Holy Roman Emperor.

Once again Frederick remained unimpressed. In February 1644 Philip IV, not having received a favourable response from the prince, turned his attention to the States-General and promised them that in return for a peace (the details of which had to be negotiated) he would send the pay of the army of Flanders in Dutch ships via Holland, thereby consenting to paying the Dutch customs duties. However, this attempt to deal separately with the prince and the States merely served to increase Dutch mistrust of Spain's intentions, and Philip's proposals were rejected.

The Spanish were once more reduced to reviewing their approach. Some of Philip's advisers thought it was time to concentrate on accommodating the French rather than the Dutch. In December 1644 Castel-Rodrigo, one of Melo's negotiators, gave his opinion that any further talks with Frederick were of no value since 'the prince mocks the king's authority and is deceiving those who are there on the part of His Majesty, diverting them with ceremonious and polite words to gain time and dispose of matters to his advantage' (**54**, p. 353). Yet there was seemingly nothing the Spanish could do to speed up the Dutch deliberations on their general peace proposals.

Even by July 1643 the Dutch provinces had not agreed either on the composition of their delegation to Münster or on its instructions. Zealand in particular proved reluctant even to enter the negotiations without first securing general agreement on the need to force Spain to concede the same fiscal regime and imposts on Flemish harbours as on Zwijn, the Scheldt and Sas. Other provinces accepted that this was a 'chief and most important' instruction for the delegates to defend, but were not prepared to commit themselves to it in the way Zealand demanded. Thus the provinces continued to debate throughout 1644. Even by April 1645, when Holland's deputies began to urge the States to send the plenipotentiaries to Münster, Zealand was still undecided: in fact, she remained opposed to the negotiations. Thus when the vote was taken to deliver the instructions to the delegates – on 28 October 1645 – there was no absolute unanimity, and when the six consenting States authorised their plenipotentiaries to leave for Münster there were vigorous protests from Zealand.

Yet Philip IV continued to hope that direct negotiations with individual States in the north would result in a settlement. Even Philip's main negotiator at Münster – the conde de Peñaranda – favoured this approach. He thought it was most important that Spain settle with the Dutch rather than the French and that prospects for this were better via The Hague than at Münster. The States-General, on the other hand, did not want to undermine its delegates in Münster and refused to countenance further direct talks at The Hague.

However, the Münster talks were soon bogged down and it took the threat of a Spanish-French treaty and the proposal that the southern Netherlands be transferred to France to shake the Dutch into considering the Spanish proposals. The talks held in May 1646 proved to be the turning point. Frederick Henry began to support the peace moves and on 13 May the Dutch delegates presented their formidable list of seventy-one conditions for a truce. Peñaranda agreed to most of them and on 30 May, after considering the Spanish response, and knowing that the thorny issue of the Indies had still to be dealt with, the Dutch agreed to move towards an agreement which was signed in July.

The relative rapidity with which the agreement was concluded alarmed the opponents of the truce in the Republic. They campaigned vigorously to block the agreement. Zealand led the opposition, but the anti-truce pamphlet campaign also had support in Friesland, Groningen and the industrial towns of Holland. The peace faction countered with a campaign of its own. Despite the colourful language of the pamphlet war, most of the provinces were unimpressed with the arguments of the opposition and deliberated not whether to overturn the truce but whether it should run for fifteen, twenty or thirty years. Holland went further and proposed that the States-General should seek to convert the truce into a full peace. The States-General debated the issue, and on 27 October

1646 it voted by six to one to support Holland's proposal. Zealand remained opposed to the move and protested that the States-General, under the terms of the Union of Utrecht, had no right to sanction action without all States being in agreement. Her protests were ignored.

The delicate negotiations focusing on colonial matters and border demarcation began in December 1646. Both sides were prepared to make concessions to prevent the talks breaking down altogether. The Dutch finally settled for Spanish recognition of their conquests in the East and West Indies, including Dutch Brazil (at its fullest extent as of 1641), and an undertaking that Spanish subjects in the Far East would not seek to extend their trade beyond the limits that then applied. The Spanish agreed to compromise over the Flemish border localities but insisted on guarantees for Catholic public worship in the new state. The points agreed in these talks, together with those settled in the previous May, were provisionally signed by the plenipotentiaries at Münster on 8 January 1647.

This signalled the renewal of opposition in the Republic to the peace [**doc. 24**], but once again it was more than matched by the propaganda of the peace faction, and even the death of Frederick Henry on 14 March did not undermine the drive for peace. Zealand expressed her opposition in the strongest terms, and Utrecht and Leiden (Holland's second city) echoed her objections. The French sought to stiffen this resistance in order to delay the return of the plenipotentiaries from Münster. France was worried that a settlement of the Spanish-Dutch conflict would allow Spain to concentrate all her attention on the Franco-Spanish conflict and she was pleased when Zealand and Utrecht forced a reopening of the Münster talks in September 1647.

However, the negotiators soon settled their differences and in November the Dutch referred all the seventy-nine articles of the draft treaty to the provinces for their approval. Utrecht and Zealand continued to oppose the draft treaty, but Friesland, Groningen, Overijssel, Gelderland and Holland approved the terms and the formal signing of the articles took place in Münster on 30 January 1648.

In general terms, by the treaty: (i) the United Provinces were recognised as independent; (ii) the Scheldt remained closed so that Antwerp remained blockaded; (iii) Dutch conquests in Flanders and Brabant were confirmed without any protection for Roman Catholic worship; and (iv) Dutch conquests overseas were also confirmed, along with the right to trade freely in both the East and West Indies.

Ratification of the treaty initially posed a number of problems, but Utrecht switched to the majority and this allowed the necessary oath-swearing to take place in Münster on 15 May. After much debate, Zealand agreed to publish the peace on 30 May, although this was more from a wish to prevent discord in the Republic than a change of heart. The peace was therefore published throughout the Republic on 5 June 1648. Only in Zealand and Leiden was there no widespread rejoicing that after eighty years the Dutch revolt was finally over.

# Part Three:  Assessment

## 9  The Economics of Revolt

> 'Let all persons know that, after a long succession of bloody wars
> ... the King [of Spain] and the States, moved by Christian
> piety, desire to end the general misery and prevent the dreadful
> consequences, calamity, harm and danger which the further
> continuation of ... wars in the Low Countries would bring in
> their train ... and to avert the mishaps, destruction and disor-
> ders which the heavy plague of war has made men suffer for so
> long and so heavily.'

Those who drafted the Peace of Münster in 1647–8 were very
clear that the Dutch war of liberation had had dire consequences
for both Spain and the Low Countries. Modern historians have
disagreed amongst themselves about whether the war *was* the
unmitigated disaster that many contemporaries thought. Some
have argued that although the economy of the southern provinces
was hard-hit by the conflict, that of the northern provinces was
given a boost by it. Others think the northern provinces did not
gain a great deal from the war while the southern provinces did
not suffer as much as has been supposed. Most argue that Spain
certainly incurred huge losses and had to make enormous sacrifices
in terms of men and resources to continue the war, and that as a
consequence it was those neutral countries on the periphery who
profited, England, Sweden and Germany, but also the bankers of
Genoa and Portugal. What sense can the student make of these
conflicting claims?

## The Dutch Republic

Defensive war can often be much more costly to finance than
offensive war. The Dutch totally rebuilt the defensive fortifications
of almost every town and then found more money to pay for
garrisons and equipment. The cost must have been enormous. Yet
in 1591 they also began to mount offensive campaigns. Little
wonder that the annual cost of the armed forces increased from 3.2

million florins in 1591 to 8.8 million florins in 1607, 13.4 million florins in 1622 and finally to 18.8 million florins in 1640 (**80**, p. 191). Such expenditure necessitated high taxation which in turn often led to social unrest and, as in Alkmaar, Haarlem, Enkhuizen and Amsterdam in 1624, open rioting. Indeed, in an attempt to avoid causing more disturbances by further tax increases, the Republic was forced to rely much more than it would have liked on raising public loans. Despite the fact that Dutch trading successes allowed the States to raise the necessary cash without increasing interest rates, by 1651 the province of Holland alone was in debt to the tune of 153 million florins.

Nevertheless, Holland seemed to do well out of the war. Large profits were made by merchants as a result of the breaking of the Spanish and Portuguese monopolies on extra-European trade and especially from cargoes of spices from Asia and sugar from Brazil. Yet figures relating to dividends paid to shareholders by the Dutch East India Company between 1602 and 1649 reveal that between 1611 and 1632 the Company only declared ten dividends in the twenty-two year period and that really large dividends were only paid after 1634. Figures showing the number of Dutch ships sailing to the East Indies between 1570 and 1670 reveal that once war was declared in 1620, the rate of growth of the East India trade slackened and did not recover until after 1649.

Trade with the West Indies was plagued with heavy losses and although the West India Company managed to declare a huge dividend of 75 per cent after the capture of the Spanish treasure fleet in Matanzas Bay, Cuba, this was almost the only dividend it ever issued. The cost of conquering and defending strongholds in Brazil more than outweighed company profits through other trading and the States General was forced to make contributions to company funds after 1623 simply to maintain a Dutch presence in this key area of South America. By 1640 the West India Company's debt was 18 million florins and gradually it lost its financial backing and was forced into liquidation in 1674. Thus the extra-European trading sector of the Dutch economy, though capable of spectacular gains, was not the overall success that some accounts have claimed. Gains were sporadic, and it is significant that only about 7 per cent of the Republic's shipping resources was ever devoted to trade with the East and West Indies.

To a very great extent the real soul of Dutch trade was the re-export of Baltic goods (especially grain and timber) to Spain and

Portugal in return for salt. This 'mother-trade' of the Dutch was much more vulnerable in wartime and was frequently disrupted by the Spanish. As Jonathan Israel has shown, after the extirpation of the Twelve Years' Truce, Spain waged economic warfare against the Republic, calculating that to undermine this vital Dutch re-export trade would quickly bring the rebels to the brink of defeat (**54**). She was right. Not only was the Dutch Baltic trade badly hit by the Spanish embargoes, but other sectors of the Dutch economy also suffered. Between 1621 and 1641 very little salt, wool, indigo or cochineal reached Holland, a state of affairs which caused rising prices and unemployment in the Republic.

When the Spanish recaptured Dunkirk in 1583 they formed a new war fleet in the port and used it to menace Dutch shipping. Privateers were attracted there and from the 1590s took a heavy toll of Dutch shipping in the North Sea. Between 1626 and 1634, 1,835 Dutch vessels were sunk or captured. These activities forced up Dutch insurance rates and convoy and escort charges. The Dutch herring fishery suffered a serious setback too, especially in the 1620s and 1630s. Gradually, after France declared war against Spain in 1635, Dutch overseas commerce recovered, and it was also helped by the rebellion in Portugal in 1640 and the outbreak of civil war in England in 1642. However, these were fortuitous circumstances and recovery was not due to any inherent benefits arising out of the Dutch struggle with Spain.

Indeed, the war served to accentuate the differences between maritime and landward provinces. The eastern provinces were involved in the fighting far longer than the western ones and large areas of farmland were laid waste and up to 20 per cent of agricultural land had to be abandoned. Population growth slowed down and in some towns, like 's Hertogenbosch, there was a noticeable decline. Even in Holland, where Walloon and Flemish refugees helped to swell numbers and provide much-needed capital investment, the growth of population slowed down (especially after the events of 1572–79). The growth of some of the main towns of Holland, such as Amsterdam and Leiden, ought not to disguise the fact that the war years did not witness a demographic boom in the Dutch Republic as a whole (**77**).

## The southern provinces

If the northern provinces experienced a slowing-down in the growth of population, the southern provinces suffered a sharp fall in population especially after the outbreak of continuous fighting in 1572. Almost every community in Flanders and Brabant lost between a half and two-thirds of its population (**81**, p. 180). As in the eastern provinces of the Republic, the rural provinces in the south suffered most. In southern Flanders during the crisis of the 1580s only about 1 per cent of the farming population remained on the land. In Brabant crops were burned and local inhabitants were terrorised by passing troops. Significantly, those provinces that returned to Spanish control in 1577–79 without fighting – Artois, Hainaut and French Flanders – escaped the devastation.

As in the Thirty Years' War in central Europe, troops of both sides in the Spanish-Dutch conflict committed atrocities and destroyed capital equipment. Local industrial production was bound to suffer as a result. The cloth works of Hondschoote were particularly badly hit, although other textile centres were also forced to cut production (and in the 1580s they hardly produced anything). Some never recovered. The heartlands of the Low Countries were ruined (**87**).

Nevertheless, as Parker has shown (**81**), the southern provinces did not remain at this low ebb for long. When the battle-lines hardened after the 1590s, more secure conditions were established and population began to increase. Antwerp in particular began to grow and once more began to trade with Italy and Spain and with non-European countries. When the Spanish troops were paid, the money often found its way to local banks, sutlers and other concerns. Hondschoote recovered by the 1620s and Ghent also began to produce large quantities of textiles. New activities, especially those concerned with quality as much as quantity (such as silk, tapestries, lace, diamond-cutting and glass-making) grew up in many towns. Profits were often used to rebuild run-down or war-damaged houses. New farming methods practically revolutionised rural Flanders by the 1640s.

However, the war continued to limit the scope of this recovery. The conflict still had to be financed and about 4 million florins a year was raised by taxation between 1600 and 1640. Troops continued to cause damage and had to be housed and fed; thus those areas close to the main fighting did not recover as quickly as other less strategic areas. Not even the Franco-Spanish conflict which began in 1635 and which brought much-needed relief for the northern provinces made any difference for many southern areas: indeed, quite the reverse. Mons in particular suffered widespread devastation and industrial collapse after 1635. Only with the industrial boom of the early nineteenth century did the southern provinces as a whole experience a recovery.

## Spain

The social costs of the war for Spain were enormous. Between 1567 and 1574 about 42,875 soldiers left Spain to fight in the Netherlands and Italy. Between 1631 and 1639 about 30,000 troops from Castile went to the Netherlands alone. Little wonder that the requirements of the army absorbed most of Spain's public expenditure. As early as 1578 Philip II lamented that the war 'consumed the money and substance which has come from the Indies, while the collection and raising of revenues in these kingdoms has only been done with great difficulty because of the dearth of specie in them (since so much is exported) and because of the damage which this does and causes to the commerce and trade on which the yield of our taxes depends'. Figures showing the amounts of money received from Castile by the Paymaster-General of the Army of Flanders reveal that there were two main periods of spending in the Netherlands corresponding to the two main Spanish thrusts in Europe under Philip II and Olivares: 1586 to 1607; and 1621 to 1640. In the period 1596 to 1600 alone, over 60 million florins were sent to the Netherlands (**81**). How did Spain manage to continue to finance her war effort?

Taxes were repeatedly increased so that by 1590 one-third of the average Castilian peasant's income was taken away as tax. When the new *millones* excise tax was introduced in the last decade of the sixteenth century, the landowners were already suffering from a fall in harvest yields. Taxation thus ran the risk of undermining the Spanish economy. To supplement income from taxation, Philip II borrowed large amounts of money and by the time of his death in 1598 the public debt had risen to 85 million ducats, having been 36 million ducats at his accession in 1557. The fastest increases in the debt corresponded to the periods of greatest expenditure on the Army of Flanders.

The cessation of hostilities in 1609 did not alleviate the financial pressures on Spain, and the government decided to continue with its recent policy of debasing the *vellón* coinage by issuing coins of pure copper instead of the normal mixture of copper and silver. In 1599 copper coins had been minted worth only a fraction of their face value. In 1603 the coins were recalled and stamped at double their value. These transactions made the government a profit of 6 million ducats, but confidence in the coinage was undermined and monetary inflation was unleashed.

The minting of *vellón* coins was stopped in 1607 after widespread protests, but it was renewed in 1617 and the government of Philip IV coined 19.7 million ducats between 1621 and 1626, to produce a net profit of over 13 million ducats. Only an increase in world copper prices slowed the minting process down. However, the damage had been done, and many foreign moneylenders, especially the Fuggers of Germany, would only lend Philip IV pure silver ducats if in return they were paid more than twice the number of *vellón* ducats. In May 1626 minting was suspended once again as the government was on the verge of bankruptcy (which was actually declared in 1627). In August 1628 the nominal value of *vellón* coins was halved.

However, money manipulation continued and a harsh inflation in 1642 practically paralysed trade. In the last years of Philip IV's reign, inflation and monetary disorder ensured that price levels in Spain were the highest in Europe. Silver had almost been driven out of circulation in Spain so that vital international payments, which were only accepted in silver, could not be made, and in October 1647 the government was forced to declare itself bankrupt for a second time.

Olivares was well aware of the fiscal pressures on the Castilian economy. As early as 1616 he had been informed that Castile was contributing 73 per cent of imperial costs, the Netherlands 9 per cent, Portugal 10 per cent, Naples 5 per cent and Aragon only 1 per cent. The injustice of this fiscal pressure on Castile encouraged Olivares, in 1626, to press forward with a scheme known as the 'Union of Arms', which aimed to force America, Flanders, Italy and the other kingdoms in Spain to contribute more to imperial defence. It was never really successful. Catalonia refused to be part of the scheme and Spanish intervention in the Thirty Years' War involving military setbacks in northern Italy (near Mantua), meant that Olivares was forced to continue to rely predominantly on Castilian resources (**33**). The pope allowed Spain to levy extra ecclesiastical taxation and this, coupled with the renewal of minting of copper coins, gave Philip IV the confidence to continue fighting the Dutch, and to help the Austrian Habsburgs in central Europe.

In fact Spain's satellites *did* contribute more in the seventeenth century, though by way of *asientos* (government contracts) and loans from foreign bankers. However, Olivares tried many other expedients. He levied 'free gifts' (*donativos*), and resumed the sale of royal villages. He encouraged Philip IV to sell about 200,000 of his subjects out of royal jurisdiction. Lesser nobles were allowed to commute their military service obligations into money payments. Sales of offices flourished, and even the national debt of *juros** was taxed. Such measures, and others, kept Spain in the Thirty Years' War and helped to finance her military presence in the Netherlands, but in Madrid there was always an atmosphere of tension at the spiralling costs.

Before bankruptcy was reached in 1647, the economy of Spain had suffered greatly. For instance, the famous wool producing areas in Old Castile were badly affected by the Spanish embargo policy, because before it was implemented most of the exported wool had been sent to the Netherlands (**87**). Indeed, those sectors that had flourished on the basis of links with the Dutch suffered real hardship after 1621. The naval blockade thus harmed many Spanish, Italian and Portuguese ports and their industries as well as the economy of the republic. It had to be partially lifted in 1629 because Flemish commerce had been so hard-hit, and it was weakened further when the Dutch drove the Spaniards from Wesel, Rheinberg, Lingen and Orsay between 1627 and 1634.

When hostilities extended along the trading routes to the New World and other non-European areas, Spain, like the Dutch Republic, had to increase spending on defence. In fact it was money well spent, since Castile lost only a few small islands in the Caribbean. Nevertheless, both Spain and the Dutch could ill-afford to spend so much money on overseas conquests or colonial defence when both domestic taxation and the level of public debt were increasing so alarmingly. Neither state could continue indefinitely to finance a conflict of world-wide proportions, which is what the revolt became after 1620. The Dutch calculated, rightly, that Spain would crack first, but it was a close-run thing.

On balance, it seems clear, as Parker has argued, that 'the prolonged conflict generated by the Revolt of the Netherlands served to retard the growth of the northern republic (and particularly of its landward provinces), to inflict permanent damage on the economy of large areas of the Spanish empire, and to ruin for two centuries the prosperity of "Belgium"' (**81**, p. 202).

# 10 Military Aspects of the Revolt

The revolt of the Netherlands lasted from the iconoclastic fury in August 1566 to the Peace of Münster in January 1648. It lasted longer than any other uprising in modern European history and involved more continuous fighting than any war of modern times – from April 1572 to April 1607 (with a six months' cease-fire in 1577), and from April 1621 to June 1647. Given the fact that the two combatants were far from equal and that, especially in the first years, the areas in revolt were small in size and population, and lacked sufficient natural resources to sustain a long war against the might of Spain, it seems remarkable that the Spaniards were unable to suppress the revolt at the outset. Parker thinks there are important logistical reasons for Spain's failure to win an early victory – the determination of the defenders and their strength by sea; the defensibility of the north-western provinces; and the diversion of Spanish resources to other theatres of operation at crucial times (**81**, p. 50).

As time passed, Spain faced two more major problems in her attempt to suppress the rebels. There were innumerable delays and difficulties caused by distance from the centre of government (which influenced the mobilisation and recruitment of troops, the ability to reinforce and relieve armies, and the control and direction of the high command). There was also the need to provide troops with all the money and munitions they required. Failure to supply soldiers with food and sufficient money led either to mutiny or mass desertion [**doc. 22**]. However, as the Spanish government soon realised, financial support had to be provided not just for a single season's campaigning, but until all the rebel strongholds had fallen [**doc. 8**].

Spain gradually came to accept that it was impossible to provide all the resources to achieve outright victory in this manner. The marquis of Aytona wrote to Olivares in 1631 outlining some of the reasons:

'If we put an army of 40,000 men in the field they [the Dutch] bring out as many and more. With that they prevent us from

doing anything. If we want to cross a river with all our main
army, they cross another with theirs. If we lay siege to one place,
they lay siege to another of ours. In this situation, Sir, in
order to get anywhere in this war it is necessary to have two
armies . . .'.

However, by 1631 the court at Madrid had long since given up
hope of winning an outright victory to end the war against the
rebels. After 1600 Spain knew she had to fight a war of attrition
until one side was financially exhausted and had to negotiate a
compromise peace. With Spain's involvement in the Thirty Years'
War after 1618, and especially with her conflict with France after
1635, it also became clear that the Dutch rebels were likely to force
Spain to the negotiating table on their terms rather than the
reverse.

## The terrain

The seaward provinces of Holland and Zealand, with their river
barriers and related obstacles (wastelands, inundations, forts and
blockhouses) were a natural 'redoubt'. The duke of Alva described
the province of Holland as 'a land of dykes, ponds and difficult
passages' (May 1573), and it proved a good base from which the
rebels could, when conditions were right, extend their territories
to include Utrecht and western Gelderland. With the river Ijssel
to the east and the multiple barrier of the Rhine and Maas (lower
Meuse) to the south, such a redoubt proved eminently defensible
(**28**, **40**).

The Dutch towns along the main rivers of the Maas, Waal, Lek
and Linge were heavily fortified, but it was not this river barrier
alone which prevented the Spanish from inflicting defeat on the
rebels. After all, both sides succeeded in crossing and re-crossing
the rivers during the wars. Rather it was the combination of terrain
and Dutch fortification which made the 'redoubt' so difficult to
penetrate. Marsh and heathland alternated with thick woods and
there were few villages along this frontier line. After 1606, when
the Dutch had reinforced this frontier with a connected chain of
blockhouses and redoubts, the Spaniards certainly found the
Republic difficult to penetrate by land. As a consequence, the
nature of the fighting changed.

Before 1600 few areas of the Low Countries were free from
intervention by enemy raiders and freebooters. Many atrocities

were committed by roving bands of soldiers who used local villages as bases to launch looting sorties into enemy territory (**37**). Thus, while there were few opportunities for pitched battles in the classical style, there was ample scope for irregular guerrilla action in the Low Countries before the turn of the century. Most of the local commanders became military entrepreneurs who planned and organised these operations. They often forced villages to pay money in return for letters of protection and they raised further money by demanding ransoms and contributions. Some commanders, like Martin Schenck in the 1580s, changed their allegiance many times in order to capitalise on changing fortunes. However, the stabilisation of the frontier in the 1590s reduced this form of private enterprise on the part of local commanders, although it did not prevent the government from issuing its own letters of protection and from annually ransoming prisoners of war (**79**, p. 18). Every military activity came to have its price.

To the south of the river network lay the great cities of Brugge, Ghent, Tournai, Valenciennes and Oudenarde, and all of them offered the rebels support at various times. The northern areas of Brabant and Flanders were easy targets for rebel armies and the ports of the Flemish coast as far south as Ostend were open to Dutch attack by sea. Even the southernmost province, Artois, was vulnerable to attack from France. Indeed, Spain could not deal with the French and Dutch at the same time, as she discovered to her cost in 1590 when Philip II was forced to commit his Dutch forces to the war in France and was unable to prevent the Dutch rebels from breaking out of their redoubt and regaining large areas of territory in the north.

The large towns of Artois, Brabant and Flanders became impressive fortresses and citadels and the Spaniards tended to attempt to reduce them by blockade rather than direct attack, or bypass them altogether. However, even the weakest of the enemy strongholds provided staunch resistance and as early as 1573 Requesens lamented:

'The quantity of rebel towns and districts is so great that they embrace almost all of Holland and Zealand, which are islands that can be reduced only with great difficulty and by naval forces. Indeed, if several towns decide to hold out, we shall never be able to take them. We who are on the spot can see all this with our own eyes, but the people at the Court of Spain have a dim and distant view'.

The rebel towns that stood next to the sea or tidal rivers, or which stood on non-tidal rivers but had a tributary which flowed near the walls, perfected a series of 'water manoeuvres' to flood Spanish siege approaches. The cutting of a dyke or the opening of a sluice at an important point in a siege could totally undermine the opposition. Even where such tactics were not possible, the soggy terrain often posed serious problems for the Spaniards. The high water-table in the north-west provinces, for instance, saturated the ground to within two feet of the surface and this forced the Spaniards to construct high siege parapets or to endure 'wet ditches'. On many occasions in the winter months, the Spaniards were forced to use skates.

## The armies

Christopher Duffy has noted that 'With few and wretched troops ... fighting in a "strong" country of rivers and marshes, it was small wonder that the war in the Netherlands was conducted according to its own rules' (**28**, p. 63). Both Spanish and Dutch commanders avoided open battle: the war in the Netherlands was a war of sieges. Initially the Spanish had the help and advice of talented Italian engineers like Captain Bartolomeo Campi and Chiappino Vitelli who were skilled in the art of fortress warfare. Even so, the generals on the spot, Alva, Parma, Spinola and Maurice of Nassau tended to become their own experts in engineering affairs. This was partly because sound technical advice was not always available when required and because neither side had permanent units of engineering troops. For special purposes Spain had to recruit labour from outside the Netherlands, although Parma discovered that even his native Spanish troops would dig in return for extra pay.

Spanish commanders were disadvantaged by the lack of artillery and transport. It was particularly annoying for generals to have important artillery pieces washed away by a flood, or to be bogged down in the soggy terrain. Even so Spaniards found land transport the safest, despite its costs and difficulties. Waterways invariably swept past well-defended fortresses which had to be avoided. This often meant that the progress of a siege was held up through lack of sufficient artillery (as at Alkmaar in 1573). Spanish commanders soon realised that they could not besiege every rebel town and they tended to target those ports and towns through which the Dutch gained much-needed relief – whether in the form of trade and supplies or military support. Even then the Spaniards preferred to try and bribe a town into submission before resorting to costly siege operations.

The Dutch too had to learn from experience. They had difficulty recruiting siege and fortress labour, but they developed their skills at garrisoning towns through long-established militia companies and guilds and the recruitment of paid garrison troops (*waardgelders*). This *waardgelder* system relieved the regular Dutch troops of garrison duty and provided them with a reserve in times of siege. The Spaniards had nothing to compare with this. Also, the Dutch found it easy to transport their heavy equipment by water. Although towns were often unwilling to let their cannon be used by the field armies, Dutch generals gradually collected a quantity of artillery and kept it in the frontier fortresses under the command of a *Meester-Generaal* to be deployed by river as and when it was required.

As might be expected, given the intense parochialism of the Dutch provinces, throughout the revolt individual provinces were reluctant to make financial contributions towards constructing or maintaining distant fortresses, especially if such fortresses did not directly serve their interests. Two provinces might contribute towards a fortress which defended their joint interests, but this was never a popular or even a common form of financing defence [**doc. 9**].

Maurice of Nassau and his cousins William Louis and Count John II of Nassau made every effort to reform Dutch military tactics in order to match Spain's Army of Flanders (**75, 96**). They stressed better use of manpower with shallower formations and reductions in the size of tactical units. They accepted the need for more officers, musketeers and arquebusiers, and perfected the manoeuvre known as the counter-march whereby successive musketeer ranks advanced, fired and retired to re-load. They also encouraged the massing of artillery to enable barrages to be employed at sieges; greater standardisation in weapon designs; the use of maps and field glasses; more attention to the training of soldiers and their discipline; and regular and better pay for soldiers.

There is no doubt that these reforms transformed the Dutch rebels into a fighting force to be reckoned with and enabled them to stiffen their resistance to Spanish offensives (**55**). However, it would be wrong to think that such methods were revolutionary. Spanish and Dutch commanders tended to make reforms where they saw positive advantages in doing so rather than cling to any single pattern of thinking. For instance, to cope with local conditions in the Netherlands, Spanish commanders often encouraged the reduction in numbers of the famous *tercio* in order to increase the frontage and reduce the depth of the formation, and to make it more flexible than the traditional unit. Not surprisingly in a terrain where fortress warfare was the norm, cavalry tactics were little changed by the Dutch, and Spanish commanders saw no real need to make great changes to this arm of their fighting forces until 1642, when in response to outside pressure Spanish cavalry companies were grouped into regiments of horse.

There were many support services in operation before the Dutch reforms. In the 1530s new Spanish recruits were sent to Italy and North Africa before being posted to the Netherlands in order to gain experience and basic training. There was also a special Spanish military treasury, a hierarchy of judicial courts, a system of medical care with resident doctors in every regiment, and a chaplain-general with a large number of chaplains under him.

Certainly the war between Spain and the Dutch rebels provided a sound training ground for many of the commanders of the Thirty Years' War and the English Civil War. It is also true that the Dutch moves of 1595 towards standardisation and uniformity in the size and calibre of weapons were of lasting importance to the conduct of war. The many Dutch military training manuals, such as the books of Jacob de Gheyn and Jacob von Wallhausen, were also influential outside the Netherlands. Yet even by 1630 the Dutch reforms had not been fully appraised in all aspects of warfare and many of the changes were not applicable to other theatres of war. 'New' methods existed side by side with older ones even in Dutch armies, and more than one commander hit upon almost the same device for solving problems that were faced by all. This was particularly true of fortress warfare.

## Fortress warfare

Although some Dutch towns had been unprotected by bastions in the early years of the fighting, by 1600 all the important towns were fortified in the style of the *trace italienne*. The bastion was a projection from the main line of the walls with four faces – two pointed outwards to face the enemy, and two at right angles to the main wall to provide a cross-fire. Gradually the height of these bastions was reduced and the walls were made essentially of brick and rubble, because it was discovered that squat brick constructions absorbed cannon-shot much better than taller stone ones. However, for much of the sixteenth century most Dutch constructions were basically earthen defences. Sometimes walls and bastions were surrounded by deep moats and often protected by further constructions and outer walls.

Spanish generals found it almost impossible to capture a town defended by the *trace italienne* in the time-honoured way of the heavy artillery bombardment to make a breach, followed by a massed assault. Such towns could only be captured by total blockade, which meant the besiegers had to construct and man a circle of fortifications around the town. Often there were two lines of fortifications for the blockade: the circumvallation (facing the country to combat any attempt by the enemy to relieve the siege) and the countervallation (to keep up a bombardment against the bastion) (**123**, Ch. 1).

Both the Dutch and the Spaniards contributed in equal measure to the major advances in fortress warfare which were made in the sixteenth and early seventeenth centuries. In the 1580s Parma had begun to construct labyrinthine siegeworks and Maurice of Nassau copied many of his ideas. When the Dutch developed some of these ideas further, the Spanish were quick to emulate them and apply them to their own fortifications, often with the help of renegade rebel engineers.

However, despite the revolutionary idea of the *trace italienne*, rebel fortifications were developed to cope with the flat terrain and the high water table of the northern provinces of the Netherlands. They had to be easy to construct and not very expensive. They employed the earthen rampart and the wet ditch and eventually incorporated elaborate outworks and regular squat bastions. Maurice of Nassau developed the complete earthen fortress at Coevorden (an example of this type of fortress still exists at Heusden). Such fortifications provided defence in depth but they had a number of weaknesses. They required a large garrison to man the walls and ramparts and once the besieger captured the outer fortifications he could use them with profit against the defenders. Wet ditches, while they were an obstacle to the attacker, were also a hindrance to the defenders in that they made the relief of outer areas difficult. In winter, most of the ditches were frozen and this tended to negate their defensive properties. The whole system depended on the site being level with a water-table just below the surface, and the wooden palisades and earthen slopes required constant attention and maintenance. The 'Dutch system' was essentially a network of field fortifications which did not require permanent masonry. As such, although Dutch ideas were exportable, their particular type of fortification was not a sound investment for other Europeans.

Although the Spanish found siegework a very time-consuming affair, they gradually learned to build impregnable attacking fortifications in order to starve the towns into submission and to undermine the morale of the inhabitants. The Dutch copied these tactics in turn when they blockaded towns controlled by Spain. Indeed, there were very few unsuccessful sieges in the Netherlands after 1622 [**doc. 23**].

Once the blockade circles of fortifications had been constructed, the attacking army began its slow march towards the town walls. Often all that was needed for a successful siege was time and sufficient resources to maintain the blockade. As the besieging army moved forward, it would construct square redoubts to act as safe bases for further progress. From these bases, at night workers ('sappers') and their protective infantry units would make their way to a forward position and begin to construct further trench fortifications and parapets. Gradually these trenches were extended towards the fortress, often in a zig-zag fashion. Where such trenches had to be constructed over marshy ground their foundations had to be laid with bundles of boughs, brush and faggots, not simply to stem flooding but also to provide a suitable passageway for equipment. Obviously, the defenders used all their cannon and armoury to break up this form of encroachment and many sorties were made to kill the workmen and destroy their work. Not surprisingly, as the trenches got nearer the fortress, the workers had to be paid more. Only when the trenches came to within thirty feet or so of the walls were the sap workers considered to have completed their task, and, after constructing musketry positions, other troops attempted to press home the attack, supported all the time by artillery fire of various kinds.

The main siege gun battery (*batterie royale*) was usually placed on a raised area about 400 or 600 paces from the fortress, and as many as thirty pieces, placed in line, would keep up a constant fire from this area throughout the siege. At times, this *batterie royale* was supplemented by smaller batteries sited on either side which concentrated on setting up a cross-fire. Commanders gradually changed their views about the best position of these batteries, and by the seventeenth century it was thought essential to place the guns no more than 200 paces from the target so that a combined trench and artillery attack could be launched on the bastions.

The Spanish also reduced the calibres of their cannon to four: the forty-eight pounder ('whistler' or 'wall-basher'); the twenty-four pounder demi-cannon; the ten or twelve pound quarter cannon; and the five or six pound eighth cannon. One of the advisers who pressed for this reform, Diego Ufano, thought that 'there was such diversity and confusion among the old pieces that it cost a good deal of trouble and effort to obtain their ammunition. Nowadays [1613] we have but a single range of artillery, all based on the full cannon and its fractions down to the eighth'. These four artillery pieces were supplemented by the mortar, which was first used in the Netherlands at the siege of Wachtendonck in 1588.

However, the long series of campaigns which began in 1621 totally lacked the urgency and drive of the first bout of wars. Innovation and technical progress suffered as a result. Technical education in Spain was limited to a small number of private schools and few of the pupils entered public service. The military reforms of 1633 reduced the number of engineers required for the artillery to six men, and the Spanish in the Netherlands were forced to rely on native masters, many of whom went to Spain to help with military engineering in the Peninsula. Thus, the Spanish were unable to institutionalise their experience of fortress warfare in the Netherlands.

Since the existence of the Dutch Republic was not really at stake after 1621, the Dutch lacked the enterprise to break out of their redoubt. Aggressive strategies were incompatible with their policy of *guerra defensiva**. Consequently the land struggle was reduced to a contest along the southern approaches to the Maas-Waal river line. Siege operations were predictable, vast and tedious, only rarely punctuated by exciting moments as when the Spanish reduced Breda in 1625. The Dutch commander after 1626 was Frederick Henry of Nassau, half-brother of Maurice of Nassau. He earned the title of 'Conqueror of Towns' for recapturing a number of towns after Spinola's departure in 1626 and for his campaigns with the French after 1635 which eventually led him to recapture Breda in 1637. Even so, Frederick Henry did little more than launch brief sorties into Spanish Flanders and there was never much doubt that the 'obedient provinces' of the south would remain in Spanish hands.

# 11 Political and Constitutional Issues: was the Dutch Revolt a Revolution?

Perez Zagorin has claimed that 'the Dutch republic was the first new state of modern times whose independence was born and forged in revolution' (**120**, vol. 2, p. 87). This revolution 'was of lengthy duration, regionally dispersed, and punctuated by intervals of repression and temporary pacification' but it was a single continuous phenomenon: 'The revolt of the provinces must be seen and analyzed as a total movement carried forward from its inception by a continuing, unbroken determination to withstand Philip II's government' (**120**, vol. 2, p. 89).

Geoffrey Parker has argued that the revolt was a series of separate revolts: a political and religious one against the new Spanish system in 1566–67, which was cruelly repressed by Alva in 1567–68; the attempted invasions – by the Sea Beggars and by William of Orange – in 1572; and a more or less national reaction to Alva's rule and the Spanish mutinies of 1576 (**80**). Taking a long-term view, Parker suggests that the moment of unity in the 1570s and 1580s was just an interlude: 'If we look back to the Middle Ages we find . . . division between centralisation and the guilds, democracy and oligarchy. We find it again in the seventeenth century and we find it . . . in the *Patriotten* of the 1780s and 1790s. I wonder whether, if we looked at it with enough detachment, we might not see the Dutch Revolt . . . as just an interlude in a much longer development'.

J. W. Smit has suggested another interpretation. Rather than a single 'revolution' or a series of revolts, Smit has pictured 'a number of revolts representing the interests and the ideals of various social, economic and ideological groups: revolts which sometimes run parallel, sometimes conflict with one another, and at other times coalesce into a single movement' (**103**). Thus, in Smit's opinion, the revolt was not inspired by a single grievance or dominated by a single social group, but rather was fed by the interests and ambitions of different groups and thus defies simple all-embracing explanations. Students of the Dutch Revolt are faced, therefore, with the important question: how far was the revolt of the Netherlands a *revolution?*

Some historians who support the idea that the Netherlands rebellion constituted a revolution have asked a further question: was it a conservative or modern revolution? Those who describe the revolt as conservative (such as Fruin, Huizinga and Geyl) argue that the main actors in the drama lacked both a radical vision of the future and a commitment to progress, change and innovation. The revolt was characterised more by the ideals of the past – the preservation of old privileges and medieval liberties – than by those of a revolutionary future. On this view, it was the centralising, absolutist government that embodied the new forces of the time. On the other hand, those who describe the revolt as modern (such as Enno van Gelder) point to the fact that the rebellion brought forth a new political order which foreshadowed later constitutional regimes in Europe. Resistance to absolutism *was* modern and the resistance in the Netherlands gave birth to a new state which eventually won its independence.

However, as Zagorin has pointed out (**120**, vol. 2, p. 90), such a debate is futile in that 'conservative' and 'modern' were inextricably interwoven in the events of the rebellion. Inevitably the circumstances of the time drove the rebels towards change: in defending their inherited order against arbitrary rule they created a federal structure of government which was a combination of the old and the new. The debate also begs the question as to whether such change *amounted* to a revolution.

## Did the States-General of the Netherlands become revolutionary in the sixteenth century?

Charles V was never allowed to forget that as ruler of the Netherlands he needed the consent of representative assemblies to impose taxation, and the support of the grandees to govern the provinces effectively. He had to swear to uphold provincial privileges and knew that he could only effectively legislate where his ordinances were in step with provincial laws. The system of local assemblies supplemented by the central States-General worked well when the States felt their representations about major policy decisions were listened to and when the high nobility were regularly consulted.

Yet there had always been areas of friction between ruler and States, not least because exasperated governments, anxious about payment of troops in the face of external attack, found the decision-making process so cumbersome and slow that they were often tempted to take short-cuts. Margaret of Austria's style of government, as regent, was certainly belligerent in relation to the States, but she followed Charles V's advice 'at all times to summon the grandees ... to the Council ... to communicate all matters to them, and not to transact any business without their knowledge'. This often created a tension between the grandees and the States, a tension which Charles V sometimes exploited to curb the influence of the States. In 1531, for instance, the emperor formally sanctioned the special role of the grandees in central government by establishing a Council of State in which they were dominant. Although Mary of Hungary (regent 1531–55) did not use the Council of State as much as Margaret of Austria (regent 1507–15 and 1518–30), and although she tried to restrict the Stadholders' powers, she nevertheless consulted with the grandees as and when occasion demanded, ever aware that she could not rule effectively without their support.

The crisis of 1557 reveals something of the pragmatic nature of relations between government, the States-General and the grandees (**39**). In 1557 economic depression, coupled with famine prices and the spiralling costs of the war with France, led to a cash-flow crisis on the Antwerp money market, and the government was forced to declare a moratorium on its debts. However, there was no rebellion because the government called the States-General and allowed it to discuss the financial crisis, and although the assembly harshly criticised the king's policies, it nevertheless granted the government an *aide* of 800,000 florins per year for nine years.

However, Granvelle persuaded Philip II that the States-General represented a danger to royal power and that it should not be summoned again. Not surprisingly, this view was opposed by the States and provincial governors who feared that Philip and Granvelle sought to undermine their traditional powers and privileges by leaving effective authority with the king in Madrid. This opposition came to regard the calling of a States-General as vital for the defence of provincial liberties and for settling the country's problems. Yet, as Smit has shown, the fact that the opposition concentrated its attacks on Granvelle should not hide the fact that the States-General and high nobility were often uneasy allies (**99**). The campaign to dismiss Granvelle reveals important insights about the nature of the political situation in the Netherlands immediately prior to the revolt.

# The campaign to dismiss Granvelle

While Charles V was able to extend his territories in the Nether-lands he was able to extend government activities, which meant that many of the leading families were rewarded for government service. In the 1550s, however, shifts in the pattern of trade led to financial difficulties and an end to the expanding territorial patronage for the monarchy. With the injection of religious emotions into politics, the new conditions in the Netherlands made the personality of the ruler more important. When, for whatever reason, confidence in the ruler collapsed, different sections of the elite, and especially the more ambitious personalities like Orange, Egmont and Hornes, were driven to safeguard their positions. Some attempted to expand their own local power base; others tried to gain more control of the central government. A few wanted to do both. Yet such activity was not seen as being anti-monarchical or treasonous; it was more concerned with problems associated with the distribution and control of patronage (**62**, Ch. 5).

Collapse of confidence in the ruler occurred in France and Scot-land as well as the Netherlands, and it was always likely to happen with a disputed succession, or with the succession of a child or a woman and the establishment of a regency. When Philip II appointed Margaret of Parma as regent for the Netherlands he did not appreciate the problems that this would cause, but Granvelle certainly did, and that is why he sought to gain control of the distribution of government patronage. Granvelle also encouraged the establishment of an inner advisory committee for the regent which would bypass the Council of State and thereby undermine the influence of leading nobles. Granvelle managed to get himself appointed as archbishop of Mechelen by persuading Philip II that it would be a fitting public recognition of his services, but knowing also that it would prevent a grandee from holding this key appoint-ment in the new system. Orange and the other provincial gover-nors were right to suspect that Granvelle's policies were designed to undermine the power of the States-General and in particular that of the grandees.

Significantly, Granvelle and Orange remained on amicable terms until 1561 because they were prepared to make deals between themselves about how patronage should be distributed. Only by mid-1561, when Orange felt he could no longer trust Granvelle to deal fairly with the nobles, did a serious break ensue.

Thus it was Granvelle's control of patronage, rather than his attempt to undermine the influence of the States-General, which led leading nobles to seek Granvelle's dismissal. As Koenigsberger says, the grandees decided they 'could not afford to play second fiddle to a jumped-up civil servant from Franche-Comté' (**62**, p. 102).

Over the next two years both sides built up their clienteles, with Orange aiming to attain a position similar to that of the Guises* in France. This meant gaining a decisive voice in government in order to control central and local patronage and to gain support in the country. Most of the provincial governors were unscrupulous in their attempts to do this. Orange tried to become 'First Grandee' of Zealand and then, more importantly, *ruwaad* or governor of Brabant. Granvelle warned Philip II that this position would make Orange supreme in a province that had not normally been administered by a provincial governor.

Granvelle's great fear in 1563, when Orange, Egmont and Hornes threatened to resign from the Council of State (though not, significantly, from their provincial governorships) unless the cardinal was dismissed, was that one of them would make himself leader of the heretics. He was alarmed by events in France, where the Edict of Amboise had granted French Calvinists a limited degree of toleration and favoured the Huguenot nobility. Granvelle warned Philip II that if Orange became governor of Brabant he would have more power in the province than Philip himself (who held the title of duke of Brabant). This battle for power in the Netherlands forced Orange to be guarded in his letters to the king since he did not want to appear disloyal. However, Orange knew that he had to control the machinery of government and this necessitated summoning the States-General more, perhaps, than he would have liked in normal circumstances (and certainly more than Granvelle desired).

Orange was never really trusted by the States-General and nor were the more unscrupulous grandees. The duke of Aerschot in particular mistrusted Orange's dealings with Granvelle before 1561, and, as the main source of patronage in the Walloon provinces, he was afraid his own political influence would be undermined.

The struggle for power also embraced the towns, though neither Orange nor Granvelle were particularly successful here. Both attempted to gain influence in town councils by seeking the election of placemen-magistrates and clients, but most councils retained their independence and avoided committing themselves to either side (**111**).

Philip II regularly sacrificed his viceroys in other dominions in order to keep the loyalty of local political elites and when he assented to Dutch demands to remove Spanish troops, shelve the bishopric scheme and recall Granvelle, it appeared that this traditional pattern of Spanish policy was to be adopted in the Netherlands. The grandees expected to control policy through the Council of State and to influence the distribution of patronage. When it became clear that this was not to be the case, the nobles were less inclined to tackle the other problems besetting the Netherlands. The Compromise and the iconoclasm of 1566 appeared to herald revolution. Yet nothing of the kind occured.

## 1566

Despite the violence of the iconoclasts and the veiled threats of the members of the Compromise, there was no large-scale popular revolt in 1566 and no coherent political programme. Where Protestants took over cities it was in order to defend themselves against government attack. The majority of the grandees and the patricians in the towns were frightened by such events and sought to restore law and order as quickly as possible. Significantly, the States-General refused to get involved and Margaret of Parma secured more support than she could claim before. Thus if a revolution occurred in the Netherlands, it was not in 1566. Did it occur, as a number of accounts claim, in 1572?

## Alva and 1572

There is no doubt that Philip II's decision to send Alva to suppress the Sea Beggars and to deter Orange from invading, though greatly dependent on court politics in Madrid (**64**), presented the Dutch with their greatest challenge, since Alva's regime sought to impose royal authority at the expense of provincial laws and the powers of representative States. Yet the ensuing struggle, involving armed rebellion and foreign intervention, did not constitute a revolution.

In July 1572 the States of Holland met at Dordrecht with the aim, as Article Eight makes plain, of re-establishing their old rights:

'His Grace [i.e. the Prince of Orange] has no other purpose than to see that, under the lawful and worthy government of the King of Spain, as Duke of Brabant, Lorraine, and Limburg, Count of Flanders, Holland, Zealand, etc., the power, authority and prestige of the Estates may be restored to their former state, in accordance with the privileges and rights which the king has sworn to maintain in these countries' [**doc. 10**].

However, by Article Nine the States were encouraged not to enter into agreement with the king or his representatives 'without securing His Grace's advice, consent, and agreement upon it'. Orange in turn promised not to act without the approval of the States. The question of where sovereignty was to be found was thus blurred. The Dordrecht assembly further confused matters by recognising Orange as Governor of Holland, though the king had already removed him from the post. This appeared to be an unprecedented interference with the royal prerogative (**99**). In the following months, the States of Holland busily set up committees to supervise or actually administer the province and to organise the war effort. Yet did these developments constitute a revolution?

Individual towns often refused to co-operate with the committees, especially over taxation. When Orange proposed that the States should take over the whole government of the province in order to force the towns to comply, they declined to do so and began instead to scrutinise the prince's own position and powers. Clearly the States wished to retain close control over the executive and a say in appointments, and they were not prepared to let Orange have sovereign power. The question of who held ultimate sovereignty was still confused and it is not certain that the States, in defending their ancient rights and privileges, had made revolutionary changes.

## The peace talks at Breda (1575) and the revolt of 1576

Philip II's representatives at Breda offered the rebels a complete amnesty and the opportunity for the Protestants to emigrate, and promised the States that as soon as peace was declared the king would summon a States-General. What was not negotiable was the king's sovereignty. In reply, the representatives of the States of Holland recognised the king's sovereignty, but claimed that as the king's advisers they had the right to suggest changes and amendments to his ordinances on all matters. While there were many amongst them who wanted to retain full sovereignty for the States, this was not proposed at the talks. The aim was clearly not to force a formal recognition of independence from Philip II but to obtain a guarantee that the rights of the States, and particularly of the States-General as the central advisory assembly, would not be distorted by Madrid or Alva's 'Spanish' administration. In this they were hardly pursuing a revolutionary line.

In the summer of 1576 the king's authority in the whole of the Netherlands collapsed. On 5 September 1576, rebel troops from Brabant arrested the Council of State in Brussels and the States of Brabant and Hainaut summoned a States-General with the aim of negotiating peace with the States of Holland and Zealand. With the support of the duke of Aerschot, who became leader of the purged and reconstituted Council of State, a peace was concluded in the Pacification of Ghent (8 November 1576). Though it is arguable that these were revolutionary acts, the States-General and the Council of States were not seeking political or religious revolution, but a return to the government as it had been under the 'late emperor Charles V, of glorious memory'. Philip II's authority was still explicitly, if ambiguously, recognised.

With the Governor-Generalship of Don John of Austria, a new attempt was made to 'reduce to obedience' the rebel provinces and cities, and this forced the States-General to appoint a rival Governor-General, the Archduke Matthias. There is no doubt that this represented a break with the past, but the States continued to claim that Matthias acted in the name of the king, despite the many restrictions they placed on his powers. Under the new arrangements, the States-General and provincial States could assemble as often as they liked and the central assembly was to make all important decisions and shape legislation on taxation, war and peace.

Significantly, support for the new arrangements came from those who had most to lose in political terms by returning to 'obedience' to the king: the rebel grandees, the regent class of the towns, and the respectable burghers and citizens' guards. The unorganised groups, such as the fishermen, sailors, dock workers and other labourers, were not allowed to participate in politics. Though Orange tried to widen the base of support for the new regime, the regents forced the States-General to reject his proposals. Even here, then, with the question of sovereignty still blurred and the lack of a popular groundswell of support for the regime, it can hardly be claimed that a revolution had occurred. Indeed, those provinces who reconciled themselves to the king in the Treaty of Arras (May 1579) were allowed to preserve the gains that the States-General had achieved up to that point (which included the Pacification of Ghent) – a clear indication that the king did not perceive these developments as revolutionary.

## The Union of Utrecht (1579)

Perhaps more than any other document, the Union of Utrecht has been seen as marking the formal establishment of the United Provinces, providing for an interlocking of sovereign states, with ultimate sovereignty depending upon the unanimous support of the constituent parts. Yet even here the claims for revolution have to be diluted. In the event of disagreement on vital issues, the various Stadtholders were to have the power to make a final decision. If agreement was still not possible, the Stadtholders were empowered to 'name impartial assessors or deputies of their own choice, and the parties shall be held to accept the decisions made by the stadtholders in this manner'. It is clear that the Union was not meant to be the basis for a new state, and the arrangements were considered to be merely temporary ones dictated by the war. There was little clarification of the powers of Philip II, and certainly no formal renunciation of the king's authority.

This last was rectified in 1581, though in terms hardly less confusing as far as the location of sovereignty in the Netherlands was concerned. In the Act of Abjuration the rights of the community against the prince were clearly adumbrated: '. . . subjects are not created by God for the sake of the prince . . . but rather that the prince is established for his subjects' sake (for without them he would not be a prince)'. If the prince did not uphold the rights of his subjects, then he forfeited their respect and obedience. The document then declared that the States-General no longer recognised the authority of Philip II 'in any matters concerning the principality, supremacy, jurisdiction, or domain of these Low Countries, nor to use or permit others to use his name as Sovereign Lord over them after this time' [**doc. 13**]. Yet the States-General still considered an outside agency essential to guarantee traditional rights and liberties, and they placed themselves first under the leadership of the duke of Anjou, and then that of the earl of Leicester.

In their early negotiations with Elizabeth, it was clear that the Dutch hoped that she would become their sovereign and protectress. However, although Elizabeth was prepared to provide military assistance, and to send Leicester as the general of the English army, she did not want to complicate an already complex constitutional situation in the Netherlands by accepting the role of sovereign and protectress. The States accepted this, but still felt it necessary to shower Leicester with honours and titles on his arrival in the Netherlands [**doc. 17**]. Elizabeth was furious. She did not want to be involved in the affairs of the Netherlands more than was necessary, yet the action of the States made it appear that Leicester was *the queen's* governor. In fact the States were at pains to point out that *they* had appointed Leicester and that he was to be *their* governor and not Elizabeth's. Whilst this episode caused some confusion and misunderstanding, it was clear nevertheless that for the first time the States openly accepted that they possessed sovereignty.

However, once in the Netherlands, Leicester hoped to establish himself as undisputed leader in the Council of States and to centralise government. He and his supporters were in favour of reforms which were detrimental to the autonomy and superiority of the States. Thus, when Leicester was called back to England in November 1586, the States began to undermine the authority of the Council of State. This development led some members of the Council to question the authority of the States. The States were forced to defend their actions, and in their written response they attempted to demonstrate how, through the urban administrations, together with the nobles, they had possessed real sovereignty for the previous eight centuries. As Kossman and Mellinck claim, this stand 'constituted the logical conclusion to the development of Dutch political thought during the Revolt.'

Yet it is also clear that the intention of this stand was not revolutionary. The States wanted to preserve intact age-old rights and privileges (universally symbolised by the Joyous Entry of Brabant, the famous charter of 1356 which every duke had to swear to observe at his 'joyous entry' or accession). By cutting their connections with Philip II the northern provinces were hardly fomenting revolution; they were opting for the traditional and familiar.

Under the new regime, each of the seven provinces had sovereign power within their respective boundaries, and each sent a delegation to the States-General which was more a meeting of allies than a parliamentary assembly. After the departure of the earl of Leicester, the States-General did not legislate on domestic matters.

# Part Four: Documents

**document 1**
## Description of the Netherlands in the seventeenth century

[The Netherlands] are a general sea-land, the great Bog of Europe. There is not such another marsh in the world that's flat. They are an universal quagmire: epitomiz'd, *A green cheese in pickle*. There is in them an aequilibrium of mud and water . . . They are the ingredients of a black-pudding . . . Even their dwelling is a miracle: They live lower than the fishes, in the very lap of the floods, and encircled in their watery arms. The waters wall them in, and if they set open their sluices, shall drown up their enemies.

Owen Feltham, *A Brief Character of the Low Countries*, 1648.

**document 2**
## Philip II's view on the religious question in the Netherlands prior to the iconoclastic fury

If possible I will settle the religious problem in those states [i.e. the Netherlands] without taking up arms, for I know that to do so would result in their total destruction; but if things cannot be remedied as I desire without recourse to arms, I am determined to take them up and go myself to carry out everything; and neither danger [to myself] nor the ruin of these states, nor of all the others which are left to me, will prevent me from doing what a Christian prince fearing God ought to do in his service, [and for] the preservation of the Catholic faith and the honour of the apostolic see.

Letter to Pope Pius V, 1566, Parker (**79**), p. 32.

**document 3**

## The first petition (or 'Request') of the nobles, presented to Margaret by Henry Brederode on 5 April 1566

We are not in doubt . . . that whatever His Majesty formerly ordained and now again ordains regarding the inquisition and the strict observance of the edicts concerning religion, has some foundation and just title and is intended to continue all that the late emperor, Charles – blessed be his memory – decreed with the best of intentions. Considering however that different times call for different policies, and that for several years past those edicts, even though not very rigorously executed, have caused most serious difficulties, His Majesty's recent refusal to mitigate the edicts in any way [the king's letter from Segovia], and his strict orders to maintain the inquisition, and to execute the edicts in all their rigour, makes us fear that the present difficulties will undoubtedly increase. But in fact the situation is even worse. There are clear indications everywhere that the people are so exasperated that the final result, we fear, will be an open revolt and a universal rebellion bringing ruin to all the provinces and plunging them into utter misery . . . [The edicts] are the source and origin of all difficulties; thus His Majesty should be asked kindly to repeal them . . . we implore His Majesty very humbly that it may please him to seek the advice and consent of the assembled States-General for new ordinances and other more suitable and appropriate ways to put matters right without causing such apparent dangers.

We also most humbly entreat Your Majesty that while His Majesty is listening to our just petition and making his decisions at his good and just pleasure, Your Majesty may meanwhile obviate the dangers which we have described by suspending the inquisition as well as the execution of the edicts until His Majesty has made his decision. And finally we declare with all possible emphasis before God and men that in giving this present warning we have done all we can do according to our duty, and state that if there should occur disasters, disorder, sedition, revolt or bloodshed later on, because no appropriate measures were taken in time, we cannot be criticised for having concealed such an apparent abuse.

Kossman and Mellinck (**63**), pp. 63–4.

**document 4**
## William of Orange encourages resistance, 1568

*William of Orange was forced into exile after his defeat in 1568, but he often wrote to his supporters in the Netherlands encouraging them not to accept the promises of the duke of Alva, or trust the Spanish administration. This extract, from a pamphlet of 1568, is typical of Orange's writing at this time.*

Open your eyes and consider the present situation more closely. If you sift out all the deeds and acts of one party and the other, you shall undoubtedly find the truth to be that all the vices with which those tyrants attempt to slander and traverse the holy, reasonable and necessary enterprises of those who for the true service of God, the king and the fatherland and the deliverance of you all, courageously endanger their lives, property and wealth, are in fact their own vices. It is they who must be blamed for deeds by which they openly disgrace themselves. You well know that by the king's own proper consent you are freely released from the oath of obedience you owe to him, if he or others in his name infringe the promises and conditions on which you have accepted and received him, until finally every right has been restored. I also remind you that according to your privileges you are permitted to close the gates of your towns and to resist by force not only the servants of your prince but also the prince himself, in person, whenever he attempts to proceed by force of arms.

Kossman and Mellinck (**63**), p. 87.

**document 5**
## Orange outlines his aims, 16 June 1572

*Once William had been forced back into the 'redoubt' of Holland and Zealand he knew that he needed the full support of the rebel States, and he outlined his aims and ideas in a pamphlet. These are some extracts from it.*

I have only the following objectives in this war:

That with full respect for the king's sovereign power, all decrees contrary to conscience and to the laws, shall be annulled and that every one who so wishes, shall be free to adopt the teaching of the prophets, of Christ and the apostles which the Churches have taught until now and that those who reject these doctrines may do so without any injury to their goods as long as they are willing to behave peacefully and can show that they did so in the past.

That the name of the inquisition shall be erased for ever . . .

That those who have no right at all to be in this country and, of course, are not allowed to oppress the souls of our humble people by force of arms, shall be banished.

That people be given back their houses, possessions, hereditary estates, their good name, their freedoms, privileges and laws, by which liberty is maintained.

That state affairs shall be discussed in the States of the provinces in accordance with the custom of our ancestors.

That political matters will be dealt with by the king himself and by the States which are chosen in every province and not be dispatched secretly by hired foreigners through whose faithlessness and greed the present troubles have come about . . .

I pray you once again, because of the loyalty which you and I owe to our dearest fatherland, that with my help you rescue, take back and protect what you don't want to lose for ever. If you do not do so, then I assert most solemnly that it will not be my fault if severer measures are taken. But if you take my admonition to heart (and I sincerely hope you will do this for your own sake) then swear allegiance firstly to Christ the only God our Saviour, next to the king who takes delight in the sworn laws, finally to me as patron of the fatherland and champion of freedom.

Kossman and Mellinck (**63**) pp. 96–7.

## document 6
## Philip II refuses to concede toleration, 1585

*Here Philip II informs his nephew, Parma, that there can be no concession to heresy.*

In spite of everything I would regret very much to see this toleration conceded without limits. The first step [for Holland and Zealand] must be to admit and maintain the exercise of the Catholic religion alone, and to subject themselves to the Roman Church, without allowing or permitting in any agreement the exercise of any other faith whatever in any town, farm or special place set aside in the fields or inside a village . . . And in this there is to be no exception, no change, no concession by any treaty of freedom of conscience . . . They are all to embrace the Roman Catholic faith and the exercise of that alone is to be permitted.

Letter to Parma, 17 August 1585, cited in Parker (**80**), p. 223.

**document 7**

## Oldenbarnevelt's religious views, 1617

*In 1617 Oldenbarnevelt discussed his reasons for supporting the Remonstrants with Dudley Carleton, the English ambassador. These are Carleton's notes made after the conversation.*

He [Oldenbarnevelt] said that the strongest, soundest and richest part of the country were papists, another great part were Lutherans, some were [atheists] and very many here in Holland Anabaptists . . . The Protestant part was not the third of the inhabitants and was divided betwixt those he termed puritans and double-puritans (for such he said he held them in England) . . . Above all things he wished to avoid the division or separation of churches which if there was no remedy must be yielded unto. He foresaw schism and, from schism, faction and confusion. The professed religion in these provinces, he said, was without order or rule or any form of government . . . Since the framing of the truce he with others had endeavoured to bring the church here under the like government as was exercised in England, France, Geneva, Germany and other reformed churches which could not be done but by giving the like authority to the States-General and to the particular towns, as was acknowledged in other places of the same profession in religion . . . In the end of our discourse he professed his own opinion was clear in the point of predestination wherein he was satisfied in his youth at Heidelberg and therefore he was contrary in judgement touching this particular to Arminius, but seeing that the government of the state [i.e. the Holland estates] had judged both opinions to be tolerated he could not but stand for the maintenance of their authority.

Rady (**93**), p. 82.

## Alva's need for resources, 1577

*The duke of Alva wanted to continue the war despite the bankruptcy of 1575. However, as this letter makes clear, he was aware of the enormous provisions this policy would require.*

This Flanders question has become very difficult to settle by force. By 'difficult' I mean it will take a long time if we are to proceed by measuring His Majesty's forces against those of his rebels. And more than anything else a quick conclusion will be promoted by the authority of the provisions which His Majesty is now arranging and the foreknowledge of those which are in preparation. That is the spirit and soul of this matter. If the provisions are cut up into instalments and reduced, all spirit and vigour will be removed – which is the exact opposite of what is required.

Letter to Mateo Vázquez, 11 September 1577, Parker (**79**), p. 238.

**document 9**
## The States of Brabant decry the ill effects of particularism, 1584

*The prince of Parma's campaign of 1584 concentrated on starving out the main towns on the river Scheldt and its tributaries and then those of Brabant. Many towns surrendered before a shot was fired. This angered those who fought to the last and were not relieved. Here the States of Brabant complain to the States of Holland about this.*

Everyone knows the excellent resources . . . which God has put in our hands to safeguard our liberty, to protect us one and all against the attack of our enemies, to reconcile our religious quarrels and end them with honour. How many admirable oaths, alliances and unions have we formed and sworn to! If they have not born fruit, the reason is clearly that each province, preferring its own particular interest, has scarcely bothered about the fate of its neighbours and allies, thinking it enough to make fine promises on paper without following them up or giving them any effect . . . That is how the fair and powerful province of Flanders has been lost.

Parker (**80**), p. 216.

## document 10
## Confusion concerning sovereignty in the Netherlands, 1572

*Contemporaries were confused about the nature of the revolt and its true implications in terms of political organisation. The pressure of events produced pragmatic solutions. Here William of Orange proposes a number of ideas to a meeting of the States of Holland at Dordrecht in 1572. The question is: where in all this is sovereignty to be found?*

They [the estates of Holland] shall discuss and ordain the best and most suitable means of restoring and re-establishing in their old form and full vigour all the old privileges, rights and usages of the towns, which may have been suppressed and taken away by Alva's tyranny . . . His Grace has no other purpose than to see that, under the lawful and worthy government of the King of Spain, as Duke of Brabant, Lorraine and Limburg, Count of Flanders, Holland, Zealand, etc., the power, authority and prestige of the Estates may be restored to their former state, in accordance with the privileges and rights which the king has sworn to maintain in these countries. And without the estates, His Grace shall not endeavour to do or command anything that concerns the provinces or that may be harmful to them . . . His Grace binds himself to undertake or command nothing without the advice or consent of the estates or at least the majority of them, and without consulting these estates and countries if and when they desire this. To this end, the estates and the delegates of the towns shall swear to His Grace to be faithful to him for ever and not to desert him, but to assist him in every possible way.

Rowen (**98**), pp. 44–5.

## document 11
## The Peace of Arras, 1579

*Early in 1579 the three southern provinces of Hainaut, Artois and Walloon Flanders seceded from the States-General and established their own Union of Arras. The Union negotiated a peace with the new governor, the duke of Parma, whereby it recognised the authority of Philip II and Parma in return for certain concessions.*

His Majesty shall send out all Spanish, Italian, Burgundian and other foreign troops not acceptable to the country within six weeks of publication of the present treaty or earlier ... During the time until the departure of the said foreigners, His Majesty and the United Lands will raise an army of natives of this country and others acceptable to His Majesty and to the estates of the provinces ...

His Majesty will choose for his Council of State ten or twelve persons, including lords and nobles as well as men of learning, all natives of the country, of which two-thirds shall be acceptable to the estates of the said provinces ...

All correspondence and dispatches shall be drawn up according to the advice and decisions of the councillors of state.

These provinces shall henceforth not be burdened in any way with taxes, tributes or impositions other than those which were in force during the time of the late Emperor Charles, and with the consent of the estates of each province respectively. Each and all of these shall be maintained in their privileges, usages and customs, in general and individually. And in the event that any be infringed, it shall be made good and restored.

Rowen (**98**), pp. 71–2.

**document 12**

# Oath of installation drawn up by the States-General for the duke of Anjou and agreed in a treaty of alliance, 19 September 1580

*The novelty of the treaty with Anjou should not be underestimated. The deputies of the States-General had always defended their rights and privileges in much the same fashion as is outlined here, but the subsequent rejection of Philip II was not based on any defined right to choose a replacement. On the contrary, a prince had the privilege to claim time to put things right. Even with Anjou's oath, there is no mention of the right to replace a prince, and this indicates how unclear the States-General was on the issue of sovereignty.*

And should it be that we, our heirs or successors, should by our own action or that of others violate [the above listed privileges] in whole or in part, in whatsoever manner, we consent and concede to our aforesaid prelates, barons, knights, cities, franchises and to all our subjects aforesaid, that they need not do us, our heirs or successors any services, nor be obedient to them in any other things we might need or which we might request of them, until such time as we shall have corrected the mistaken course hitherto pursued toward them, and have completely abandoned and reversed it.

Griffiths (**45**), p. 348.

## Act of Abjuration, 1581

**document 13**

Let all men know that, in consideration of the matters considered above and under pressure of utmost necessity . . . we have declared and declare hereby by a common accord, decision and consent the king of Spain, *ipso jure* forfeit of his lordship, principality, jurisdiction and inheritance of these countries, and that we have determined not to recognize him hereafter in any matter concerning the principality, supremacy, jurisdiction or domain of these Low Countries, nor to use or permit others to use his name as Sovereign Lord over them after this time.

26 July 1581, Rowen (**98**), p. 102.

## An Englishman's opinion of the Duke of Anjou, 1579

**document 14**

His inconstant attempts against his brother; his thrusting himself into the Low Country matters; his sometimes seeking the King of Spain's daughter, sometimes your Majesty [Elizabeth I]; are evident testimonies he is carried away with every wind of hope, taught to love greatness any way gotten, and having for the motioners and ministers of his mind only such young men as have shown they think evil contentment a sufficient ground of any rebellion; whose age gives them to have seen noe other commonwealth, but in faction; and divers of which have defiled their hands in odious murders. With such fancies and favourites, is it to be hoped for that he will be contained within the limits of your conditions? Since, in truth, it were strange, he that cannot be contented to be second person in France and heir [presumptive], would come to be the second person in England, where he shall pretend no way sovereignty.

Letter from Sir Philip Sidney to Queen Elizabeth I, 1579, Holt (**50**), p. 124.

**document 15**
# Henry III of France promises to support Anjou in the Netherlands

*This general promise of French help disappointed the States-General because
it implied that Henry would not help Anjou until such time as peace was
restored in France. However, it sustained Dutch hopes that the Anjou alliance
would, in the end, encourage Henry to declare war against Spain.*

I will aid and assist you will all my power, and I will join, league,
and associate myself with the provinces of the Netherlands that
have contracted with you, once they have effectively received and
admitted you to the lordship of the said provinces, following your
request to me. I hope that God will have the goodness to restore
my kingdom to peace before then.

Henry III to Anjou, 26 December 1580, Holt (**50**), p. 141.

**document 16**
# Catherine de Medici's fears about a Spanish war, 1580

I will begin by telling you, my son, that no mother who has ever
desired the union and welfare of her children, as I surely do even
more than the preservation of my own life, has been more relieved
and contented than I with the complete satisfaction that the king
has had with you and your laudable behaviour in this pursuit and
negotiation of peace ... But having heard ... that you now
demand the king to help you in this matter with men and money,
I must confess that my joy has changed to utter perplexity. Moreover, I have no doubt whatsoever that this project will not only
deprive you of the glory and recognition that you have earned by
your service to the king and this kingdom in the matter of the said
peace, but it will also ruin the House [of Valois], bring you public
hatred and ill will, and completely destroy this state. In short it
will leave me the most distressed and troubled mother who was
ever born ... The king your brother has always told you that he
truly desired to contribute to your grandeur and advancement. But
this was something that he could not do until he had first restored
peace to his kingdom ... Moreover, my son, do not you find it
pertinent that you and the king your brother should undertake this
war against the most powerful prince in Christendom, before you

have even ascertained for sure the will and friendship of your neighbours, especially those who have a vital interest in the hegemony of the said catholic king, such as the queen of England and the German princes? . . . My son, you made all those negotiations without us, to my great regret, and it does not follow that you should place this kingdom in danger, destroy it, and displease the king your brother simply to keep your word.

Letter to Anjou, 23 December 1580, Holt (**50**), p. 143.

## document 17
## The States-General bestows titles and honours on the earl of Leicester, February 1586

*By resolving to grant Leicester these titles and honours, the States-General openly accepted that they possessed sovereignty, and that Leicester was to be their own, not Queen Elizabeth's, governor.*

His Excellency (in addition to the title, charge and commission given him by Her Majesty, and in addition to the authority which he possesses by virtue of the Treaty concluded between Her Majesty and the above named States-General . . .) shall be commissioned Governor and Captain-General of the aforesaid United Provinces . . .; and that His Excellency . . . shall have full power and absolute command in the matter of the war and all matters concerned with it . . . His Excellency shall have full and absolute power in the aforesaid Provinces and associated regions, in the matter of civil government and justice, such as the Governors-General of the Netherlands have in all times legally possessed, and particularly in the time of Charles V of beloved memory . . . And his Excellency shall be empowered to summon the States-General of the said Provinces at any time and place within the said Provinces, or wherever he wishes; and on the summons of His Excellency they shall be bound to appear at the designated time and place. In addition, the said States, both general and particular, shall assemble when they wish and act as they deem proper for the welfare and service of the country: All this without prejudice to the rights, freedoms, preeminences, privileges, treaties, contracts, statutes, ordinances, decrees and customs of the above-mentioned provinces in general, or of each province, city and member of each in particular, which, notwithstanding anything above, shall remain in their full vigour.

Griffiths (**45**), pp. 528–31

**document 18**

## Three views of William of Orange

(i) The Prince of Orange is a dangerous man, sly, full of ruses ... seeking only the favour of the populace; appearing sometimes Catholic, sometimes Calvinist and sometimes Lutheran. He is capable of any underhand deed that might be inspired by an unlimited ambition.

Cardinal Granvelle in a letter to Philip II, 1563.

(ii) He blamed the Calvinists as provoking sedition and strife, yet he spoke with horror of the edict that sentenced them to death ... In short, the Prince would have liked to see established a fancy kind of religion of his own, half-Catholic, half-Lutheran, which would satisfy both sides. Indeed, if you look at his inconsistency on religious questions, you will see that he put the state above the Christian religion.

Pontus Payen, *On the Civil War in the Low Countries*, c. 1590.

(iii) Orange was not a doctrinaire revolutionary intent on founding a new political and social order but a prudent, highly practical, and occasionally unscrupulous statesman. As the almost perfect incorporation of the sixteenth-century idea of a *politique*, he readily changed his political and religious affiliations when it suited his purposes. Yet there was one cause which he embraced with grim determination and to which he remained wholeheartedly committed until the end of his life: the struggle against the king of Spain in order to ensure that justice be done to himself and other victims of Spanish tyranny. It was on this issue that he rejected the idea of compromise and felt more strongly than almost any of his supporters.

Swart (**102**), p. 38.

# The truce between Spain and the Netherlands

*Clause Four of the truce between Spain and the Netherlands agreed in 1607 and confirmed by Madrid in 1609. This proved to be one of the more contentious clauses of the agreement.*

The subjects and inhabitants of the countries of the said lord king, archdukes and estates shall have good relations and friendship with one another during the said Truce, without resenting the damage and harm that they have received in the past; they shall also be able to enter and to stay in one another's countries, and to exercise there their trade and commerce in full security both by sea and other waters as well as by land; however, the said king understands this to be restrained and limited to the kingdoms, countries, lands and lordships which he has and possesses in Europe and other places and seas in which the subjects of other princes who are his friends and allies have the said trade by mutual consent; as regards the places, towns, ports and harbours that he holds beyond the said limits, that the lords estates and their subjects may not carry on any trade without the express permission of the said lord king; but they shall be allowed to carry on the said trade, if it seems good to them, in countries of all other princes, potentates and peoples who may wish to permit them to do so even outside the said limits, without the said lord king, his officers and subjects who depend on him making any impediments in this event to the said princes, potentates and peoples who may have permitted it to them, nor equally to them [i.e. the Dutch] or to the persons with whom they have carried out or will carry out the said trade.

J. Dumont, *Corps Universal Diplomatique de Droit de Gens*, vol. v, part 2, Amsterdam, 1728, pp. 99–102.

# The truce damages Spain and divides the Netherlands

*In Spain the debate over whether or not to renew the truce and on what terms began in March 1618. Here the secretary to the Council of State, Juan de Ciriza, advises ministers that if the truce is to be continued, it needs to be improved.*

According to our information from Flanders, for several years the Dutch have been divided into parties: the maritime towns want war on account of their interest while the rest press for peace so as to be free of the taxes and burdens that war brings. Also it has been seen throughout that the truce was highly favourable to the Dutch and that since it was signed, they find themselves unhindered with overflowing wealth while these realms are much diminished, since the Dutch have taken their commerce, and that this damage, if not remedied, will daily become worse.

2 March 1618, cited in Brightwell (**13**), p. 277.

**document 21**

## Spain lacks confidence, 1619

*Philip III's Chief Minister, Baltasar de Zúñiga, assesses Spain's situation in 1619.*

. . . We cannot by force of arms, reduce those provinces to their former obedience. Whoever looks at the matter carefully and without passion, must be impressed by the great armed strength of those provinces both by land and by sea, their strong geographical position ringed by the sea and by great rivers, lying close to France, England and Germany. Furthermore that state is at the very height of its greatness, while ours is in disarray. To promise ourselves that we can conquer the Dutch is to seek the impossible, to delude ourselves. To those who put all blame for our troubles on to the Truce and foresee great benefits from breaking it, we can say for certain that whether we end it or not we shall always be at a disadvantage. Affairs can get to a certain stage where every decision taken is for the worse, not through lack of good advice, but because the situation is so desperate that no remedy can conceivably be found. However it is also certain that, from the present Truce, which has not been properly applied as regards the Indies, have arisen those damaging consequences which we see. For this reason we must take more adequate measures in future.

Zuniga to Juan de Ciriza, 7 April 1619, Brightwell (**13**), p. 289.

**document 22**

## Mutiny was a financial disaster for Spain

*Requesens is here reported as laying the blame for Spain's ills in 1574 on the shoulders of the mutineers.*

I was forgetting to tell you a dreadful and most unworthy thing that His Excellency [Requesens] said to me: he insisted that it was not the prince of Orange who had lost the Low Countries, but the soldiers born in Valladolid and Toledo, because the mutineers had driven money out of Antwerp and destroyed all credit and reputation, and believed that within eight days His Majesty would not have anything left here ... Despair motivates desertion.

Hernando Delgadillo to Juan de Albornoz, 9 July 1574, Parker (**79**), p. 185.

**document 23**

## Attacking forces gain the upper hand in sieges

*Marshal de Tavannes, a writer on siege warfare in the seventeenth century, notes the implications of the improved 'scientific' form of attack as initially worked out by Spinola and Maurice of Nassau.*

Thirty years ago [he was writing in about 1620] fortresses were so well provided with defences that in the prevailing ignorance of the time [they] were regarded as impregnable, and even those which were very weak were not at all easy to capture ... Nowadays the besieger has gained the upper hand, and the defence of fortresses has been so weakened that we can see that without the help of an entire army, and not just small detachments, they have no hope of holding out ... Nowadays the Spanish and Dutch officers have made the capture of towns an art, and they can predict the duration of resistance of a fortress, however strong, in terms of days.

Tavannes, *Mémoires de Tres-Noble et Tres-Illustre Gaspard de Saulx, Seigneur de Tavannes*, in *Nouvelle Collection*, 1st series, Paris 1850, p. 178; cited in Duffy (**28**), p. 100.

**document 24**

## Dutch opposition arguments against the peace arrangements, 1647

*The break-through at Münster in May 1646 provoked the opponents of a Spanish settlement within the Republic to mobilise every means to wrest the initiative from the peace supporters and block the truce. Most of the arguments appeared in popular tracts, like this one.*

It is everywhere known ... that by peace or truce the common man in the enemy's provinces will greatly increase his prosperity and business, while the common man here will largely be stripped of his trade and manufactures, since many store-keepers who during the war have their goods manufactured here, will then have them manufactured in Flanders and Brabant to obtain them cheaper ... and that when the Flemish sea-ports are opened not only will consumption of our manufactures greatly decline in all lands but so will price-levels because their goods are manufactured more cheaply than ours ... and that the inhabitants of Brabant and Flanders will no longer obtain their foodstuffs and French, Spanish, Italian, Irish, Scandinavian, and Baltic wares through these lands but directly by sea, all to the detriment of the ordinary man here.

J. I. Israel (**54**), p. 363.

# Glossary

*Anabaptism* As an organised movement Anabaptism had its origins in Zurich where Conrad Grebel and others began to demand a more radical reformation than Zwingli. The distinctive features of Zurich Anabaptism were: the acknowledgement of no authority other than the Bible; the true church consisted only of the 'saints' who had undergone spiritual conversion (a conviction which led adherents to support adult baptism, a feature which gave the movement its distinctive name); withdrawal of the 'saints' from the secular community (which meant refusal to take part in government and a refusal to obey man-made laws). These beliefs soon found favour with many oppressed groups in Europe. For many authorities, there was a clear link between Anabaptism and political radicalism and this led to persecution. In the Netherlands, Menno Simmons organised a less radical form of Anabaptism in the name of 'Congregations of Christ'. The 'Mennonite Movement', as this form of Anabaptism came to be known, increased its influence until William of Orange granted it freedom of worship in 1577.

*Brethren of the Common Life* A community in the Netherlands formed by Gerard Groote. Groote preached spiritual communion with God and a devotion to education and care of the poor. There were two branches to the movement: one which went in the direction of regular monasticism with men like Thomas à Kempis arguing that a Christian's life should be modelled closely on that of Jesus; the other which developed into lay monasticism which was concerned with the quality of a Christian's life on earth and took its inspiration from the Bible.

*Council of Trent* A General Council of the Church which was convened by the Pope in December 1545 in the small imperial city of Trent in the southern Alps. It was convoked in order to establish some authoritative definition of doctrine at a time when the line between orthodoxy and heresy was difficult to draw. By the time the council had completed its work eighteen years later, about 270 prelates had taken part in its deliberations and a host of reforming decrees had been issued. The Tridentine decrees (as the Trent

135

decrees were called) did not transform the Catholic Church overnight, but the council did mark a turning point in the history of the Roman Church, giving Catholics a certainty about their beliefs and practices which the Reformation had undermined.

*Devotio Moderna* A particular type of Christian humanism developed in the Netherlands by the Brethren of the Common Life. It was a movement which reacted against the formal style of theology of the scholastics and emphasised instead the importance of spiritual communion with God.

*Duke of Buckingham* (George Villiers, 1st Duke of Buckingham, 1592–1628). He supported James I's plans for a marriage alliance between Prince Charles and the Spanish Infanta. He accompanied Charles on an unsuccessful journey to Spain in 1623 and subsequently favoured war against Spain in the Thirty Years War. He also supported the marriage of Charles to Henrietta Maria (sister of Louis XIII of France), but aroused the opposition of Parliament by promising concessions to English Catholics in 1624. He organised an alliance with the United Provinces in 1625, but subsequent lack of success in the war against France led to him being singled out by the opposition in Parliament as 'the cause of all our miseries'; he was assassinated by John Felton in 1628.

*Guerra defensiva* Tactics and strategy in war geared to defence rather than attack.

*The Guise family* The Guises became prominent in French life in 1527 when Francis I made Claud of Lorraine a duke and peer of France. Claud's son, Francis, second duke of Guise, became Lieutenant-General of the kingdom under Henry II. He saw it as his duty to protect France not only from foreign enemies but also from those 'enemies' within France who sought to undermine the power of the Catholic Church and the authority of the king. Thus he detested the French Protestants (Huguenots) and particularly the House of Bourbon which was closely linked with the new religion.

*Juros* Spanish annuities on state revenues, sold by the crown for ten to fifteen times their yearly value as a means of raising revenue quickly, but which in practice increased the king's debts.

*Lepanto* At a time when the duke of Alva was in control of affairs in the Netherlands, Philip II diverted resources to the Mediterranean as part of a plan to defeat the Turks. Philip appointed his half-brother, Don John, to command his fleet and in October 1571

Spain resoundingly defeated the Turks in the Gulf of Lepanto near the Greek mainland. The Ottoman navy was almost wiped out and about 30,000 Turks were killed or captured.

*Moriscos* There had officially been no members of the Muslim faith in Spain since 1526 and those who had been Muslims were now forced to be Christians (known as 'new' Christians or Moriscos). However many Moriscos retained some of the practices of their old faith and many still spoke Arabic. From time to time fears were expressed that the Moriscos would unite with Muslims in North Africa to facilitate a Muslim revival in Spain. In the early 1560s Philip II tried to impose stricter conditions on the Moriscos, but they were already being treated harshly and, in consequence, the Moriscos of Granada revolted in 1568. There was much cruelty on both sides before the revolt was suppressed in 1570. The Moriscos were forced to move away from the southern provinces to areas which were inhospitable or where the local communities were hostile. In the 1590s Spain tried to force the Moriscos to move to other countries, a policy which caused them much hardship.

*Puritans* The term is often used in a general sense to refer to all those in England (both inside and outside the established church) who believed in further reform in a Protestant direction. At first there was some uniformity in the demands of the Puritans, especially for more preaching in the Church. The ideas and policies of William Laud led many Puritans not only to attack the doctrines of the established Church but also the political system which supported Laudianism. In the period of the English Civil War and Interregnum (1642–1660), Puritans diversified into a number of sects with little unity (and with different names: Presbyterians, Independents, Baptists, Quakers, etc.).

*Ridolfi plot* During a period when relations between England and Spain had taken a turn for the worse (1568–1572), a Florentine banker named Ridolfi, who had been used by the Spanish ambassador in England as a go-between with the leaders of the Northern Rebellion of 1569, was implicated in a plot against Elizabeth I. In March 1571, Ridolfi tried to encourage the Catholic duke of Norfolk to rally all Catholics in England to rise in rebellion, seize Elizabeth and free Mary, Queen of Scots, from captivity, at the same time as a Spanish expeditionary force landed on the east coast. There was little chance that the plot would have succeeded, but it was uncovered and Norfolk was arrested and executed.

# Bibliography

The place of publication is London, unless otherwise stated.

1  Adams, S., 'Spain or the Netherlands? The Dilemmas of Early Stuart Foreign Policy', in Tomlinson, H., (ed.), *Before the English Civil War*, 1983.

2  Adams, S., 'The Lurch Into War', *History Today*, 38, May 1988.

3  Adams, S., *The Armada Campaign of 1588*, Historical Association New Appreciations in History, 13, 1988.

4  Backhouse, M., 'The official start of armed resistance in the Low Countries: Boeschepe, 12 July 1562', *Archiv fur Reformationsgeshichte*, lxxi, 1980.

5  Baelde, M., 'The Pacification of Ghent in 1576: Hope and Uncertainty in the Netherlands', *Low Countries Year Book*, xi, 1978, pp. 1–17.

6  Baelde, M., 'Financial Policy and the Evolution of the Demesne in the Netherlands under Charles V and Philip II' in Cohn, H. J., (ed.), *Government in Reformation Europe, 1530–1560*, 1971.

7  Balke, W., *Calvin and the Anabaptist Radicals*, Grand Rapids, 1982.

8  Barbour, V., *Capitalism in Amsterdam in the Seventeenth Century*, Michigan, 1963.

9  Bindoff, S. T., *New Cambridge Modern History*, Cambridge, 1958, vol. 2, pp. 50–69.

10  Boogman, J. C., 'The Union of Utrecht: its Genesis and Consequences', *Low Countries Year Book*, xii, 1979.

11  Brandt, G., *The History of the Reformation and other Ecclesiastical Transactions in and about the Low Countries*, 4 vols, 1720–30.

12  Braudel, F., *The Mediterranean and the Mediterranean World in the Age of Philip II*, 2 vols, 1972–3.

13  Brightwell, P., 'The Spanish System and the Twelve Years Truce', in *English Historical Review*, 12, no. 4, 1982.

14  Burke, P., (ed.), *Economy and Society in Early Modern Europe*, 1972.

**15**  Carter, C. H., 'Belgian autonomy under the archdukes', *Journal of Modern History*, 36, 1964.

**16**  Casey, J., 'Spain: a Failed Transition' in Clark, P., (ed.), *The European Crisis of the 1590s*, 1985.

**17**  Clark, G. N., 'The birth of the Dutch Republic', *Proceedings of the British Academy*, xxxii, 1946.

**18**  Clark, G. N., *Sir William Temple's Observations Upon the United Provinces of the Netherlands*, Oxford, 1972.

**19**  Coonan, J. S., 'The Gentry of Gelderland 1543–77: politics and the law', St Andrew's University Ph.D thesis, 1984.

**20**  Corvisier, A., *Armies and Societies in Europe, 1494–1789*, Indiana, 1979.

**21**  Crew, P. M., *Calvinist Preaching and Iconoclasm in the Netherlands, 1544–1569*, Cambridge, 1978.

**22**  Davis, K. R., 'No Discipline, no Church: an Anabaptist contribution to the Reformed tradition', *Sixteenth-Century Journal*, 13, 1982.

**23**  Davis, R., *English Merchant Shipping and Anglo-Dutch Rivalry in the Seventeenth Century*, 1975.

**24**  Deursen, A. T. van., 'Holland's experience of war during the Revolt of the Netherlands' in Duke, A. C., and Tamse, C. A., (eds), *Britain and the Netherlands: War and Society: papers delivered for the Sixth Anglo-Dutch Historical Conference*, The Hague, 1977.

**25**  Dietz, B. 'Privateering in north-west European waters, 1568 to 1572', University of London Ph.D. thesis, 1959.

**26**  Duke, A. C., 'From King and Country to King or Country? Loyalty and treason in the revolt of the Netherlands', *Transactions of the Royal Historical Society*, 5th series, xxxii, 1982.

**27**  Duke, A. C., and Tamse, C. A., (eds), *Britain and the Netherlands: War and Society: papers delivered for the Sixth Anglo-Dutch Historical Conference*, The Hague, 1977.

**28**  Duffy, C., *Siege Warfare: The Fortress in the Early Modern World, 1494–1660*, 1979.

**29**  Earle, P., (ed.), *Essays in European Economic History, 1500–1800*, Oxford, 1984.

**30**  Edwards, C. S., *Hugo Grotius: The Miracle of Holland*, Nelson-Hall, Chicago, 1981.

**31**  Elliott, J. H., 'A question of reputation? Spanish foreign policy in the seventeenth century', *Journal of Modern History*, 1983.

**32**  Elliott, J. H., *Richelieu and Olivares*, Cambridge, 1984.

**33**  Elliott, J. H., *The Count-Duke of Olivares: the statesman in an age of decline*, Yale, 1986.

**34**  Essen, L. van der., *Alexandre Farnese*, 5 vols., Brussels, 1937.

**35**  Evans, J. X., (ed.), *The Works of Sir Roger Williams*, Oxford, 1972.

**36**  Finer, E. I., 'State and nation-building in Europe: the role of the military' in Tilly, C., (ed.), *The Formation of National States in Europe*, Princeton, 1975.

**37**  Fishman, J. S., *Boerenverdriet: violence between peasants and soldiers in early modern Netherlandish art*, Ann Arbor, 1982.

**38**  Flinn, M. W., *The European Demographic system, 1500–1820*, Hassocks, 1981.

**39**  Friis, A., 'The two crises in the Netherlands in 1557', *Scandinavian Economic History Review*, 1, 1953.

**40**  Geyl, P., *The Revolt of the Netherlands 1559–1609*, 1932.

**41**  Geyl, P., *The Netherlands in the Seventeenth Century*, 1936, 1964, (2 vols).

**42**  Geyl, P., *The History of the Low Countries: Episodes and Problems*, 1964.

**43**  Grappenhaus, F. H. M., *Alva en de Tiende Penning*, Zutphen, 1982.

**44**  Griffiths, G., *William of Hornes, Lord of Heze, and the Revolt of the Netherlands (1576–1580)*, University of California Publications in History, 51, Berkeley and Los Angeles, 1954.

**45**  Griffiths, G., *Representative Government in Western Europe in the Sixteenth Century*, Oxford, 1968.

**46**  Gutmann, M. P., *War and Rural Life in the Early Modern Low Countries*, Princeton, 1980.

**47**  Haley, K. H. D., *The Dutch in the Seventeenth Century*, 1972.

**48**  Hess, A. C., *The Forgotten Frontier. A History of the sixteenth-century Ibero-African frontier*, Chicago, 1978.

**49**  Hibben, C. C., *Gouda in Revolt. Particularism and Pacificism in the Revolt of the Netherlands, 1572–1588*, Utrecht, 1983.

**50**  Holt, M. P., *The Duke of Anjou and the Politique Struggle during the Wars of Religion*, Cambridge, 1986.

**51**  Houtte, J. A. van, *An Economic History of the Low Countries 800–1800*, 1977.

**52**  Hunt, R. N. C., 'Some pamphlets of the revolt of the Netherlands against Spain', *English Historical Review*, 44, 1929.

**53**  Israel, J. I., 'A Conflict of Empires: Spain and the Netherlands 1618–48', *Past and Present*, 76, 1977.

54  Israel, J. I., *The Dutch Republic and the Hispanic World, 1606–1661*, Oxford, 1982.

55  Jesperson, K. J. V., 'Social change and military revolution in early modern Europe', *Historical Journal*, 1983.

56  Kamen, H., *Spain 1469–1714: A Society in Conflict*, 1983.

57  Keeney, W. E., *Dutch Anabaptist Thought and Practice, 1539–1564*, Nieuwkoop, 1968.

58  Knetsch, F. R. J., 'The National Synod of Dordrecht, 1578, and the Position of the Walloon Churches', *Low Countries Year Book*, xii, 1980, pp. 40–50.

59  Koenigsberger, H. G., 'The Organisation of Revolutionary Parties in France and the Netherlands during the Sixteenth Century', *Journal of Modern History*, xxvii, 1955.

60  Koenigsberger, H. G., 'The Statecraft of Philip II', *European Studies Review*, 1, 1971.

61  Koenigsberger, H. G., *The Habsburgs and Europe, 1516–1660*, Cornell, 1971.

62  Koenigsberger, H. G., *Politicians and Virtuosi: Essays in Early Modern History*, 1986.

63  Kosman, E. H., and Mellinck, A. F., (eds), *Texts Concerning the Revolt of the Netherlands*, Cambridge, 1975.

64  Lagomarsino, D., *Philip II and the Netherlands, 1559–1573*, 1988.

65  Lamet, S. A., 'The *Vroedschap* of Leiden 1550–1600: the Impact of Tradition and Change on the Governing Elite of a Dutch City', *Sixteenth-Century Journal*, 12, 1981.

66  Limm, P. R., *The Thirty Years War*, London and New York, 1984.

67  Lovett, A. W., 'A New Governor for the Netherlands: the Appointment of Don Luis de Requesens, Comendador Mayor de Castilla', *European Studies Review*, 2, 1971.

68  Lovett, A. W., 'The Governorship of Don Luis de Requesens, 1573–76: a Spanish View', *European Studies Review*, 3, 1972.

69  Lovett, A. W., *Early Habsburg Spain, 1517–1598*, Oxford, 1986.

70  Lynch, J., *Spain under the Habsburgs*, vol. 1: *Empire and Absolutism, 1516–1598*; vol. 2: *Spain and America, 1598–1700*, Oxford, 1964, 1969.

71  MacCaffrey, W. T., *Queen Elizabeth and the making of policy 1572–88*, Princeton, 1981.

72  Maltby, W. S., *Alba. A biography of Fernando Alvarez de Toledo, third duke of Alba 1507–1582*, Berkeley, 1983.

**73**  McNeil, W. H., *The Pursuit of Power: technology, armed force and society since A.D. 1000*, Chicago, 1982.

**74**  Motley, J. L., *The Rise of the Dutch Republic*, 1855.

**75**  Nickle, B. H., *The Military Reforms of Prince Maurice of Orange*, University Microfilms, Ann Arbor, 1975.

**76**  Nijenhuis, W., 'Variants within Dutch Calvinism in the Sixteenth Century', *Low Countries Yearbook*, xii, 1979.

**77**  Noordegraaf, L., ' Dearth, Famine and Social Policy in the Dutch Republic at the End of the Sixteenth Century', in Clark, P., (ed.), *The European Crisis of the 1590s*, 1985.

**78**  Parker, G., *Guide to the Archives of the Spanish institutions in or concerned with the Netherlands (1556–1706)*, Brussels, 1971.

**79**  Parker, G., *The Army of Flanders and the Spanish Road 1567–1659*, Cambridge, 1972.

**80**  Parker, G., *The Dutch Revolt*, 1977.

**81**  Parker, G., *Spain and the Netherlands 1559–1659: Ten Studies*, 1979.

**82**  Parker, G., *The Thirty Years' War*, 1984.

**83**  Parker, G., 'New Light on an Old Theme: Spain and the Netherlands, 1550–1650', *European History Quarterly*, xv, 1985.

**84**  Parker, G., and Wilson, C., (eds), *An Introduction to the Sources of European Economic History, 1500–1800*, 1977.

**85**  Peteghem, P. van., 'Flanders in 1576: reactionary or revolutionary?', *Low Countries Year Book*, xi, 1979, pp. 65–84.

**86**  Pettegree, A., 'The Strangers and their Churches in London, 1550–1580', Oxford University D. Phil. thesis, 1983.

**87**  Phillips, C. R., 'The Spanish wool trade, 1500–1780', *Journal of Economic History*, xlii, 1982.

**88**  Pierson, P., *Philip II of Spain*, 1975.

**89**  Potter, G., and Greengrass, M., *John Calvin*, 1983.

**90**  Prestwich, M., *International Calvinism, 1541–1715*, Oxford, 1985.

**91**  Price, J. L., *Culture and Society in the Dutch Republic during the Seventeenth Century*, 1974.

**92**  Rady, M. C., *The Emperor Charles V*, London and New York, 1988.

**93**  Rady, M. C., *The Netherlands: Revolt and Independence, 1550–1650*, 1987.

**94**  Ramsay, G. D., *The End of the Antwerp Mart*, vol. 2: *The Queen's Merchants and the Revolt of the Netherlands*, Manchester, 1986.

**95** Reitsma, R., *Centrifugal and centripetal forces in the early Dutch Republic: the States of Overijssel, 1566–1600*, Amsterdam, 1982.

**96** Roberts, M., *The Military Revolution, 1560–1660*, Belfast, 1956.

**97** Rodriguez-Salgado, M. J., 'From Spanish ruler to European ruler: Philip II and the creation of an empire', Hull University Ph.D thesis, 1984.

**98** Rowen, H., *The Low Countries in Early Modern Times*, 1972.

**99** Shennan, J. H., *The Origins of the Modern European State, 1450–1725*, 1974.

**100** Steen, C. R., *A Chronicle of Conflict: Tournai 1559–67*, Utrecht, 1985.

**101** Swart, K. W., 'The Black Legend during the Eighty Years War', in Bromley, J. S., and Kossmann, E. H., (eds), *Britain and the Netherlands: papers delivered at the Fifth Anglo-Dutch Historical Conference*, The Hague, 1975.

**102** Swart, K. W., *William the Silent and the Revolt of the Netherlands*, Historical Association, General Series 94, 1978.

**103** Smit, J. W., 'The Present Position of Studies regarding the Revolt of the Netherlands', in Bromley, J. S., and Kossmann, E. H., (eds), *Britain and the Netherlands: papers delivered at the First Anglo-Dutch Historical Conference*, The Hague, 1960.

**104** Smit, J. W., 'The Netherlands Revolution' in Forster, R., and Greene, J., (eds), *Preconditions of Revolution in Early Modern Europe*, Baltimore, 1970.

**105** Sutherland, M. N., *Princes, Politics and Religion, 1547–1589*, 1984.

**106** Tex, J. den, *Oldenbarnevelt*, 2 vols, Cambridge, 1973.

**107** Thompson, I. A. A., *War and Government in Habsburg Spain, 1560–1620*, 1976.

**108** Vries, J. de., 'An Inquiry into the Behaviour of Wages in the Dutch Republic and the Southern Netherlands, 1580–1800', *Acta Historiae Neerlandicae*, 1978.

**109** Wansink, H., (ed.), *The Apologie of Prince William of Orange*, Leiden, 1969.

**110** Wedgwood, C. V., *William the Silent*, 1944.

**111** Wells, G. E., 'Antwerp and the Government of Philip II 1555–1567', Cornell University Ph.D thesis, 1982.

**112** Wernham, R. B., ' English Policy and the Revolt of the Netherlands' in Bromley, J. S., and Kossmann, E. H., (eds), *Britain and the Netherlands: papers delivered at the first Anglo-Dutch Historical Conference*, The Hague, 1960.

**113** Wernham, R. B., *The Making of Elizabethan Foreign Policy 1558–1603*, California, 1980.

**114** Wernham, R. B., *After the Armada: Elizabethan England and the struggle for Western Europe, 1588–1595*, Oxford, 1984.

**115** Wilson, C., *Queen Elizabeth and the Revolt of the Netherlands*, 1970.

**116** Wilson, C., *The Dutch Republic and the Civilisation of the Seventeenth Century*, 1968.

**117** Winter, J. M., (ed.), *War and Economic Development*, Cambridge, 1975.

**118** Woltjer, J., 'Dutch privileges, real and imaginary', in Bromley, J. S., and Kossmann, E. H., (eds), *Britain and the Netherlands: papers delivered at the Fifth Anglo-Dutch Historical Conference*, The Hague, 1975.

**119** Wyntges, S. M., 'Family allegiance and religious persecution: the lesser nobility and the revolt of the Netherlands', *Sixteenth-Century Journal*, xii, 2, 1981.

**120** Zagorin, P., *Rebels and Rulers 1500–1660*, 2 vols, Cambridge, 1982.

RECENT PUBLICATIONS

**121** Kouri, E. I., and Scott, T., (eds), *Politics and Society in Reformation Europe*, 1988.

**122** Kouri, E. I., 'For True Faith or National Interest? Queen Elizabeth I and the Protestant Powers', Ch. 19 in (**121**).

**123** Parker, G., *The Military Revolution: Military Innovation and the Rise of the West, 1500–1800*, Cambridge, 1988.

**124** Stradling, R. A., ' Olivares and the Origins of the Franco-Spanish War, 1627–35', *English Historical Review*, 101, 1986, pp. 68–94.

**125** Stradling, R. A., *Philip IV and the Government of Spain, 1621–1665*, Cambridge, 1988.

# Index